To Chester ~
may you always
feel loved. You will
forever be in my heart! ♡
Love you ~
Sharon ☺
Nov. 1, 2009

Love Everlasting

The Art of Romance Through the Millennia

Flint Institute of Arts

January 29 – March 19, 2000

Published on the occasion of the exhibition
LOVE EVERLASTING: The Art of Romance through the Millennia
at the Flint Institute of Arts
January 29 – March 19, 2000

Organized by the Flint Institute of Arts
Co-curated by Raymond J. Kelly III, Guest Curator
and Kristie Everett, Coordinator of Exhibitions

Exhibition Sponsors
Founders Society
C.S. Harding Foundation
BANK ONE

Additional support has been provided by

GENESYS
HEALTH SYSTEM
Lynne M. and J. Parkhill Smith

Accredited by the American Association of Museums

Printed in the United States

ISBN# 0-939896-20-6

Flint Institute of Arts
1120 E. Kearsley Street
Flint, Michigan 48503-1991

Front cover: Benjamin West
American, 1738-1820
Romeo and Juliet
oil on canvas, 1778
50 x 44¼ inches
New Orleans Museum of Art: Museum purchase
Women's Volunteer Committee Fund, 73.33

Back cover: Niccolo dell'Abate
Italian, c. 1509-1571
Eros and Psyche
oil on canvas, c. 1560
39¼ x 36½ inches
The Detroit Institute of Arts, Founders Society Purchase, Robert H. Tannahill Foundation Fund, 65.347

Table of Contents

Acknowledgements

It is not possible to assemble an exhibition such as this without the generous participation of many wonderful individuals who were willing lend these important art works from their collections. The following people have also assisted in many invaluable ways and without their help and support this exhibition would not have been possible. I would like to personally thank Townsend Wolfe and Thom Hall at The Arkansas Art Center, Lois Zona and Rebecca Davis at The Butler Institute of American Art, David Farmer and Erica Blumenfeld at the Dahesh Museum, Stephen Bruni and Dr. Mary F. Holahan at the Delaware Art Museum, Graham Beal and Michelle Peplin at the Detroit Institute of Arts, William Eiland and Donald Keyes at the Georgia Museum of Art, Elizabeth James at C. & J. Goodfriend Drawings and Prints, Iris Krenzis Cohen at Hammer Galleries, Ivan and Ethan Karp at the O.K. Harris Gallery, Cleve K. Scarbrough, Ellen Simack, and Elizabeth Le at the Hunter Museum of American Art, Erin Brutus and Robin Blakney-Carlson at The Hyde Collection Art Museum, James Mundy and Joanne Potter at The Frances Lehman Loeb Art Center, Dana Holland-Beickert and Kip Peterson at the Memphis Brooks Museum, Charles Mo at the Mint Museum of Arts, Andrew Maass and Kathy Greenberg at the Mississippi Museum of Art, Sandra Paci at DC Moore Gallery, Malcolm Rodgers and Kim Pashko at the Museum of Fine Arts, Boston, Michael Milkovich at the Museum of Fine Arts, St. Petersburg, E. John Bullard, William A. Fagaly, and Paul Tarver at the New Orleans Museum of Art, David Ebitz and Glen Gentele at the John and Mable Ringling Museum of Art, Larry Ross, Robert Simon of Robert Simon Gallery, and Bob Jackson at Time Life Syndication, video artist Nicholas Rieben and Dr. and Mrs. Henry C. Landon, III.

This exhibition and catalogue are filled with too many details for one person or even one department to manage. Each exhibition calls for a team effort from staff and volunteers, and *LOVE EVERLASTING* was no exception. I wish to acknowledge Bryan Christie, Preparator and his assistants, Jonathan Shethelm and Lonnie Williams for their outstanding job of installing the exhibit; Melissa Farr, Curatorial Assistant, for her thorough research; Monique Desormeau, Education Curator, and Valarie Shook, Administrative Assistant, for proofreading and attention to the details of producing this catalogue; Andy Isola, Public Relations Coordinator and Dennis Ferrara, contract staff, for promoting the exhibit; and Deborah Gossel, Assistant Director for Development for her efforts in identifying funding for *LOVE EVERLASTING.*

Kristie Everett, Coordinator of Exhibitions

FOREWORD

The Flint Institute of Arts was created to collect and present the great artistic achievements through the ages from around the world. Needless to say, exhibit opportunities abound; but, with the coming of a new millennium, the idea to assemble and present an exhibition dealing with a thousand years of civilization's artistic achievements was simply irresistible. The only problem was where to begin.

In approaching such a nebulous subject, the staff began by considering the many threads of human thought and behavior that make up the complex weave of history: invention and technology, philosophy and spirituality, war and pestilence, and, of course, the compelling and inescapable manifestations of romantic love. What better subject is there to portray all ages of all cultures equally and with hopeful expectations for the next millennium than mankind's most gratifying obsession – love? Throughout history, artists from all cultures have reflected upon and idealized romantic love, portraying the amorous relationships found in mythology, literature, religion and real life experiences.

It is fundamentally human to have feelings of romantic love and essentially unavoidable to develop an appreciation for the stories of romance. All cultures, throughout history, have celebrated accounts of romantic adventures and misadventures. Often an important subject in a culture's artistic expressions, religious parables, poems, songs, and historical retelling, romance's spectrum of behavior from passion and bliss to betrayal and loss is told and retold countless times by artists, poets, philosophers, and historians.

Romance can be described as the behavior of individuals stimulated by love. Driven by the forces of attraction, desire, infatuation, passion and joyful exuberance, romance also encompasses love's expressions of devotion, sharing, trust, marriage, sacrifice, separation and even loss. Powerful and often undeniable, the compulsion to express romantic emotions of love is common to all people of all cultures around the world. From the beginning, it seems, love has made the world go 'round and has been a strong motivator of the great and notorious actions of men and women. Human history is richly embroidered with the legends of the famous and infamous romantic deeds of its heroes and heroines. Infinitely interesting, love's tales, both fact and fiction, appeal to our inherent passions and our most fundamental and often uncontrollable desires to express the urges of the mind and body. The greatest stories of romance become universal symbols of love's conquests — Adam and Eve, Paolo and Francesca, Celadon and Amelia, Oberon and Titania, Romeo and Juliet, and Rinaldo and Armeda — retold with images in this exhibition, dramatizing the common and universal expressions of love.

Romantic behavior can range from euphoria to despair. Yet, each love affair feels unique and each moment of the affair feels private and isolated from the outside world. Romantic behavior is often complex, complicated by the contradictory impulses of love, which can, at once demand and comply, lead and follow, give and possess.

Kristie Everett, FIA Coordinator of Exhibitions, researched and selected the works of art for this exhibition. Since the selections in this exhibition were felt to have appeal to a wide and diverse audience, our intent was to invite a scholar to interpret each image but in the broadest, most conversant manner. The works of art Kristie selected for this exhibit operate on many levels and were selected intentionally to portray both the diversity of subjective approaches and aesthetic evolutions. In speaking with museum patron and long-time friend, Raymond J. Kelly III, about the scope of Kristie's selections for this exhibit, I was reminded, by his observations and comments, of his remarkable background in the classics and his great ability to connect concrete and abstract ideas and articulate them. I asked R.J. if he would consider cocurating the exhibit with Kristie, and he accepted.

Raymond J. Kelly III is a graduate of Notre Dame and Oxford. He served in Army Intelligence in Berlin, Washington and Vietnam. Since 1969, he has been a stockbroker in Flint. He lives in Flushing, Michigan, with his wife, Kathleen and five children and is the son of the late Raymond and Kay Kelly who were long-time patrons and advocates of the Flint Institute of Arts. Scholar and linguist (R.J. speaks seven languages), his insightful observations of the images go far beyond mere stylistic appraisals. R.J. is not one to miss double entendre or nuance. He is able to contextualize each work of art on a brief page. In each description he captures the essence of the image's meaning and style and relates it to the era, location and inspiration of its origin. It has been a pleasure and privilege to work with R. J. Kelly and I am most grateful for the time, energy and creative thinking he dedicated to this project.

Whenever possible, the FIA endeavors to collaborate with colleagues from the culturally rich environs of the Flint area. Our neighboring cultural institutions have made *LOVE EVERLASTING* a centerpiece for their own programming revolving around the theme of romantic love. The Flint Symphony Orchestra's 1999-2000 concert season is dedicated to the symphonies written for Romeo and Juliet. The Greater Flint Arts Council's exhibit schedule is linked thematically to love with two exhibits titled *What Love Means to Me: All Members Juried Exhibit* and *Gifts of Love: Annual African-American Exhibit.* Also, two of Whiting Auditorium's winter presentations, the ballet *Romeo and Juliet* performed by Ballet De L'Opera and *The Barber of Seville* performed by the New York City Opera Company, complement and enhance *LOVE EVERLASTING: The Art of Romance Through the Millennia.*

Financial support of exhibitions through sponsorship is critically important to the success of the FIA. On behalf of the FIA, I am thankful for Wilaine Northway's efforts, who, as President of the Founders Society, provided leadership and a commitment to funding, making it possible to begin the exhibition project. I also wish to thank Claire White, FIA Trustee, and the C.S. Harding Foundation for their generosity. Bank One, through Thomas Gilbertson, President, and Ron Butler, Vice President of the Public Affairs Division, both of the Flint office, also provided financial support, without which, the exhibit would have suffered. I also wish to thank FIA Trustee Carolyn Joseph for introducing the exhibition to Genesys Health System and Tim Keener, Vice President of System Development, for the additional support Genesys provided. And finally, thank you to FIA Trustee Lynne M. Smith and her husband, J. Parkhill Smith, for their generous contribution to the exhibit.

John B. Henry III, Director

INTRODUCTION

Romantic love is the oldest of our stories. "In the beginning ... male and female He created them." In the Sumerian *Epic of Gilgamesh,* the wild and powerful savage, Enkidu, is entranced and tamed by a woman from the city. Ancient Greece told of Odysseus' longing for his wife Penelope through twenty years of war and wandering, while the Roman hero Aeneas had to reject the love of Dido before accomplishing the destiny given him by the gods. Dante, after his medieval pilgrimage through hell and purgatory, found in heaven his love of Beatrice transfigured. The story of romantic love has been told for millennia, again and again, in generation after generation; and it never fails to find its hearers.

Romantic love also is the most common of our experiences. We are born as the result of love and grow into it, from puppy love through the confusion of adolescent attractions to a marriage that is supposed to go on "happily ever after," i.e. until death. The quest for coupleship dominates the first third of our lives, its achievement sets the terms of our social interaction in the second third, and its natural end is often the striking sorrow of the last third. Its power and attraction are the measure of our clichés: "there's someone just right for you out there somewhere," "someday my prince will come," "love conquers all," "if only *he,* or *she,* or, for the truly ambitious, *they,* would call." It is our configuring metaphor — think of all the things we 'love': sunsets, puppies, a great cup of coffee, Mozart's *Jupiter Symphony,* the smell of burning leaves, a first kiss, even pop icons like Elvis.

Where do the young learn of romantic love? From images and words: from movies, magazines, MTV, from Sinatra and Sting, and sappy romance novels, from great literature and whispered gossip. Some of this learning is from ancient sources, some from those as sharp and glitzy as today. Each of the works in this exhibit was in its own time and way part of that teaching, for other generations who had to learn to love; and we present these works to contribute to that learning, through past millennia and into future centuries.

The poet or the story-teller has the luxury of showing love as a process, over time, from first stirrings and courtship through the joining of two as one to the varied ends of mature satisfaction or bitter separation or the tragic and unwanted parting of death. The visual artist, on the other hand, must capture this long process in one crucial event, freeze-frame a significant moment in this most powerful of experiences, and reduce a complex psychology of attraction and growth to an outward appearance. The eighteenth-century American painter Benjamin West does this masterfully in *Romeo and Juliet.* Shakespeare's play takes two or three hours; but West's painting shows, in an instant, the concentrated, centripetal world of the two lovers and the outside centrifugal forces symbolized by the nurse. The nurse is real, acutely aware of the dangers lurking around the couple. But the lovers ignore her warnings and concentrate only on each other. As in other famous pictures of couples — Dürer's *Adam and Eve,* Van Eyck's *The Arnolfini Wedding Portrait,* Ruben's *Self-portrait with Isabella Brant,* Gainsborough's *Robert Andrews and His Wife* — the couple exists in a world of their own.

Romantic love is not only a story; it is a process, a journey through time. 'Romantic' comes from the medieval French word for tales of chivalry, long, complicated narratives of knights on quests. Like any good story, love has a beginning, a middle and an end. If we are blessed, such a story lasts most of our lives. This exhibit intends to portray the episodes of that story.

The process begins in uncertainty and hesitation. In early adolescence, we first become aware of love's promptings, like the young girl in Bouguereau's *Whispering of Love,* which begins the exhibit. First love soon meets first heartbreak — a stage represented by Edwin Long's *Love's Labour Lost.* Rejected youth bounces back quickly and dashes down the street, kissing every available girl, like the young sailor in Eisenstaedt's famous photograph of VJ Day: "when I'm not near the girl I love, I love the girl I'm near."

Having many loves is only for the psychologically crippled Don Juan. For most, only one special person answers the demands of desire; and that part of the quest goes by the lovely, old-fashioned term 'wooing.' The term comes from an Anglo-Saxon word "of obscure origin," according to the Oxford English Dictionary — a derivation that will not surprise anyone who has gone through the experience. The exhibit has a powerful illustration by Howard Pyle that portrays a crucial moment in this step; it is called *When All the World Was Young* and shows the asking of a question. If the answer is 'no,' the time of finding love can be excruciating: who has not felt the pain shown in George Bellows' powerful *Solitude?* If the answer is 'yes,' the relationship is on a new plane, that of love returned. Ingres' *Paolo and Francesca* portrays that moment, the moment that kept those lovers together for all eternity (albeit in their case an eternity in Dante's Inferno). Rodin's *Eternal Spring* shows us the next step, sometimes a nano-second, sometimes years away: the closeness, the joining that makes the two become as one.

Romantic love is not the selfishness of lust, even if it does stop short of the altruism of selflessness. While it seeks to possess the other, it does so by wanting above all to please the other, to the point of leaving everyone else out. Gone are the Saturday night buddies, the kid sisters and younger brothers: "a man must leave father and mother and cling to his wife" (Matthew 19:5). The joining of two into one is not merely a private act. It unites families, groups of friends and (long ago and nowadays) businesses, estates, vocations and intellectual careers. The wedding celebrates that joining and puts it into the context of the many interested parties. The legal requirement that a marriage be witnessed goes back to a Reformation-era controversy over private or clandestine marriages — the sixteenth century equivalent of "I'll respect you in the morning." The social requirement, that not just two individuals but also two families, two groups of friends, two careers come together, is even older. It is deeply rooted in our need to have love affirmed by all those around us. The exhibit shows paintings of two different weddings: Stearns' *The Marriage of Washington* and Carroll Cloar's *Wedding Party.* The similarities of the two events are more striking than their differences.

After the marriage comes the honeymoon; for that, we can look at dell'Abate's *Eros and*

Psyche. The names are the Greek words for longing and soul — now happily in bed together and at ease with one another. Longing or desire seeks what it lacks, wants a completion impossible in self alone. After the honeymoon, true love will grow in unexpected ways and directions. Chagall's *Composition with Bouquet,* probably painted some years after his marriage to Bella, shows a freshness of appreciation for his wife that all married couples should learn. Then, for many, will come the mildly irritating but deeply satisfying stage of parenthood — yet another indication that true love is not just the private world of a couple. For the exhibition, a typically Victorian piece, Spencer's *Domestic Happiness,* has been selected.

Happy endings, however, are not always the outcome. Two very powerful images — Hogarth's *Marriage à la Mode,* plate II, and Guy Penè du Bois' more stolidly serious *Café Madrid* — show couples moving in different, selfish directions. The distractions of the world and the sad pleasure of loneliness are both magnets, pulling individuals away from the center. In one sense, separation is the final result of all romantic love. Even the strongest relationships are shadowed by death's inevitability — at some point everything will have its end.

Love is not only a process for an individual's growth, it is also a renewal, the human race's way of beginning again. Tonight, somewhere, an old man lies dying, while by him sits in tears the woman who has loved him for half a century. Tonight, somewhere, a couple twenty years married rises after dinner to dance; and as they hold each other the closeness of those years flood back in memory. Tonight, somewhere, a young man in blazer and tie stands at the foot of a stairs and watches the gentlest, most beautiful girl he has ever seen come down toward him. And so, somewhere tonight, one person will whisper to another "I love you," and heart's longing will be turned to joy, and the wonder will begin again.

Raymond J. Kelly III, Guest Curator

William-Adolphe Bouguereau
French, 1825-1905

Whispering of Love (Chuchotements de l'Amour)
oil on canvas, 1889
62 x 36½ inches
New Orleans Museum of Art: Gift of Mr. and Mrs. Chapman H. Hyams, 15.6

1

During the second half of the nineteenth century, William-Adolphe Bouguereau was one of the great French Academicians, the official style against which the Impressionists rebelled. This work, painted in 1889, was the height of fashion only one hundred years ago. Only in the past thirty years have the passions and fads of art criticism cooled enough to allow a fairer appraisal. Craft and a sense of composition begin to attract appreciation again, after a half-century of aesthetic and political experimentation.

The painting shows the first faint moments of the stirrings of love. A young girl sits; modest and self-contained but vaguely troubled. She stares beyond the foreground, not past the viewer but into an area without time or space. She is dressed in a chiton, the Greek robe that Bouguereau uses in the "neo-Greek" style. (Viewers of the English Pre-Raphaelites will recognize the frequent use of "neo-Greek" by such painters as Burne-Jones and Alma-Tadema.) Her elbow rests casually on a proto-geometric vase, the pottery style of Greece from the eleventh to the ninth century B.C., the age of the *Iliad* and the *Odyssey.*

Perhaps she is a fourteen year old Penelope wondering which of the young lords of Homeric Greece might win her hand. Achilles? Very handsome but distant. Menelaus? Powerful but too gruff. But certainly not Odysseus, that short, scrawny prince of Ithaca — too clever by half. Into vague thoughts a name is whispered by the fluttering Cupid, or Eros, to give him his Greek name. Both words mean longing and desire: that is what the girl hears, faintly, for the first time.

We have here the very beginnings of romantic love: young, unfocused, yearning for a dream. We know it comes in part from the biochemical changes of adolescent growth and in part because of the social role that society sets. But as Bouguereau reminds us here, it is also a mysterious stirring, a whispering in the air as we sit alone and the very secrecy of what we hear excites us to begin life's journey.

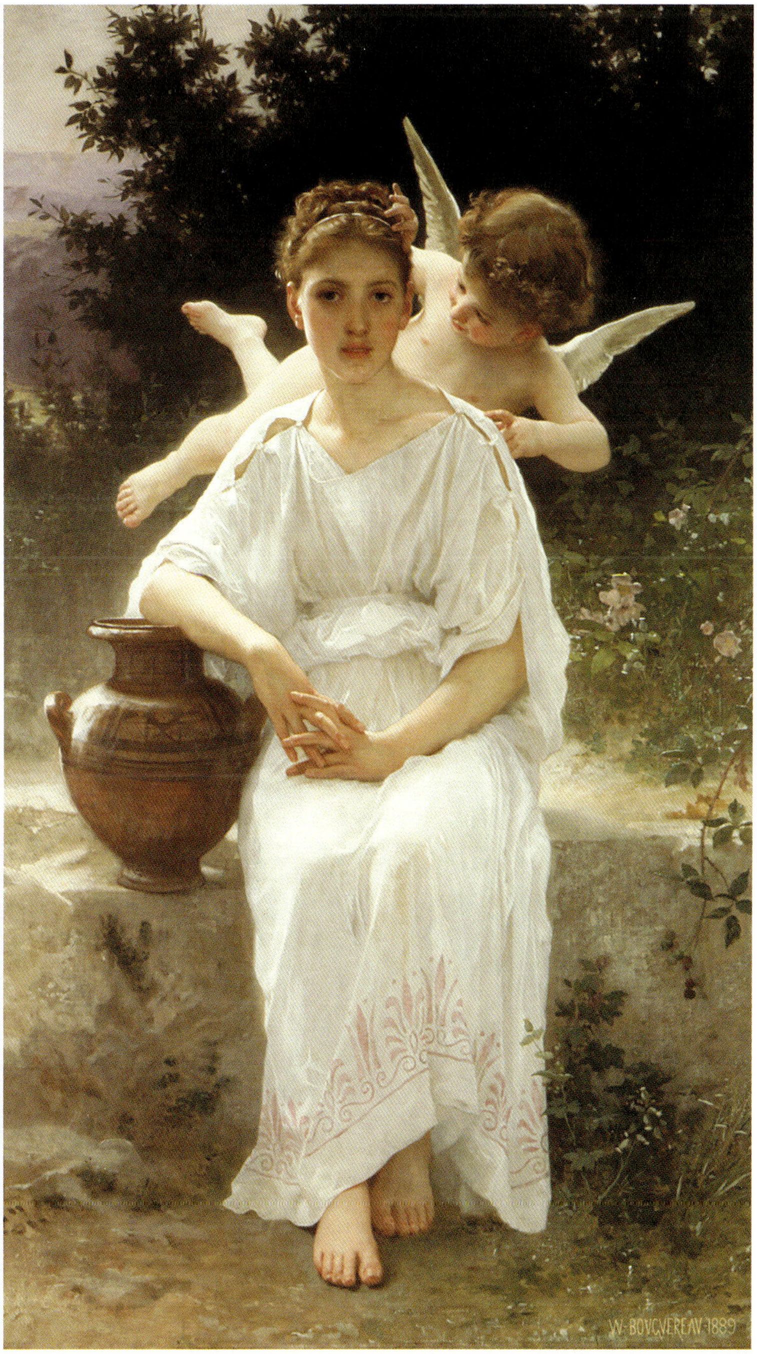
W. BOVGVEREAV 1889

Charles-Joseph Natoire
French, 1700-1777

Meeting of Jacob and Rachel at the Well
oil on canvas, 1732
39½ x 56 inches
Private Collection, United States

The twenty-ninth chapter of Genesis tells the story of Jacob's first sight of his future wife, Rachel.

There in the fields was a well with three flocks of sheep lying beside it. Jacob was still talking to the shepherds, when Rachel came with the sheep belonging to her father, Laban. As soon as Jacob saw Rachel, he kissed her and burst into tears. Now Laban had two daughters, the elder named Leah and the younger Rachel. There was no sparkle in Leah's eyes, but Rachel was shapely and beautiful.

Clearly there is a powerful attraction here between Jacob and Rachel, while the other woman on the left, possibly Leah, points to him but makes casual gossip with the shepherds. The strong emotion of the biblical account shows more in the yearning in Jacob's face and the swirl of his red garments than in his gestures. While Rachel with her hands offers herself to Jacob, his gestures offer three sheep in return.

Many nowadays read such scenes as an incident in Jewish history, the development of God's covenant with His chosen people. But for Charles-Joseph Natoire, living in a religiously rigorous France (the Edict of Nantes had been revoked fifteen years before his birth), this was equally an event in Christian history. Jacob is listed in the first chapter of St. Matthew's Gospel as third in the line of Christ's forebears, and echoes of that association resonate throughout this picture. Rachel, dressed in white and wrapped in a rich blue mantle, wears the colors of Mary. Her head is positioned well above Jacob's and all the others in the scene. Jacob bending in subservience looks like the servant he will become for fourteen years to earn Rachel's bride-price: from a New Testament perspective he prefigures Joseph, Christ's foster-father, obedient and hard-working. It is in the rippling strength of his body that we are reminded of Jacob, the patriarch-in-training. Within a few years he will become the father of twelve sons by four women, an amazing technicolor dream-coat of offspring.

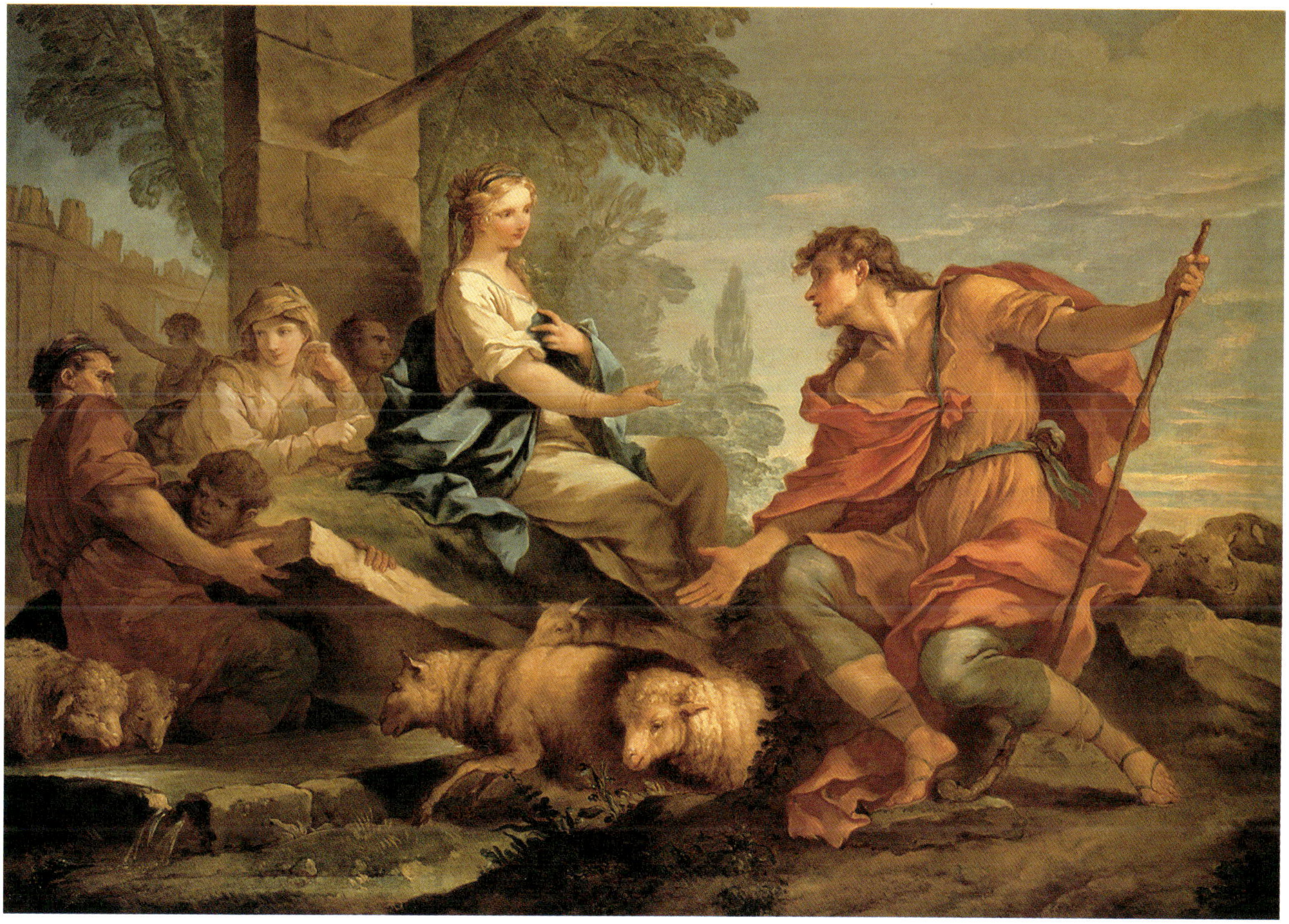

OSKAR GROSS

AMERICAN, B. AUSTRIA 1871-1936

The Automat
oil on canvas, 1915
50½ x 43½ inches
Dr. and Mrs. Henry C. Landon, III

3

In Gross' subtle rendering, two strangers sit side by side in that most New York and most impersonal of eating places, the Horn and Hardart automat. The woman sits bolt upright, rigidly straight, surprised, while the man's body is a much more dramatic diagonal slash across a full three-quarters of the painting's surface. A stripe on the wall behind them both binds their heads together and emphasizes their separation. He bends away from her, apparently focused on his food, but his right foot touches her leg.

The start of love is often a surprise: the classical metaphor of Cupid's arrows refers to an event not only sharp and painful but also fast and unexpected. She may have felt his flirtatious foot a second before; but she cannot yet choose what to say: "Excuse me!" (harshly) or "I'm sorry" (more gently) or (with a laughing trill) "I do believe that's your foot, sir" or stony silence. As they sit in their bulky coats, a moment before decision, Gross lets us imagine the next step: will it be a stern re-emphasis of winter cold or a future like Rodin's *Eternal Springtime* (catalogue no. 21).

Oscar Gross was born and first trained in Imperial Vienna in its twilight. After further study in Munich and Paris, he emigrated to New York. This work shows affinities to the mid-nineteenth century style of genre painting but with a twentieth-century New York edginess.

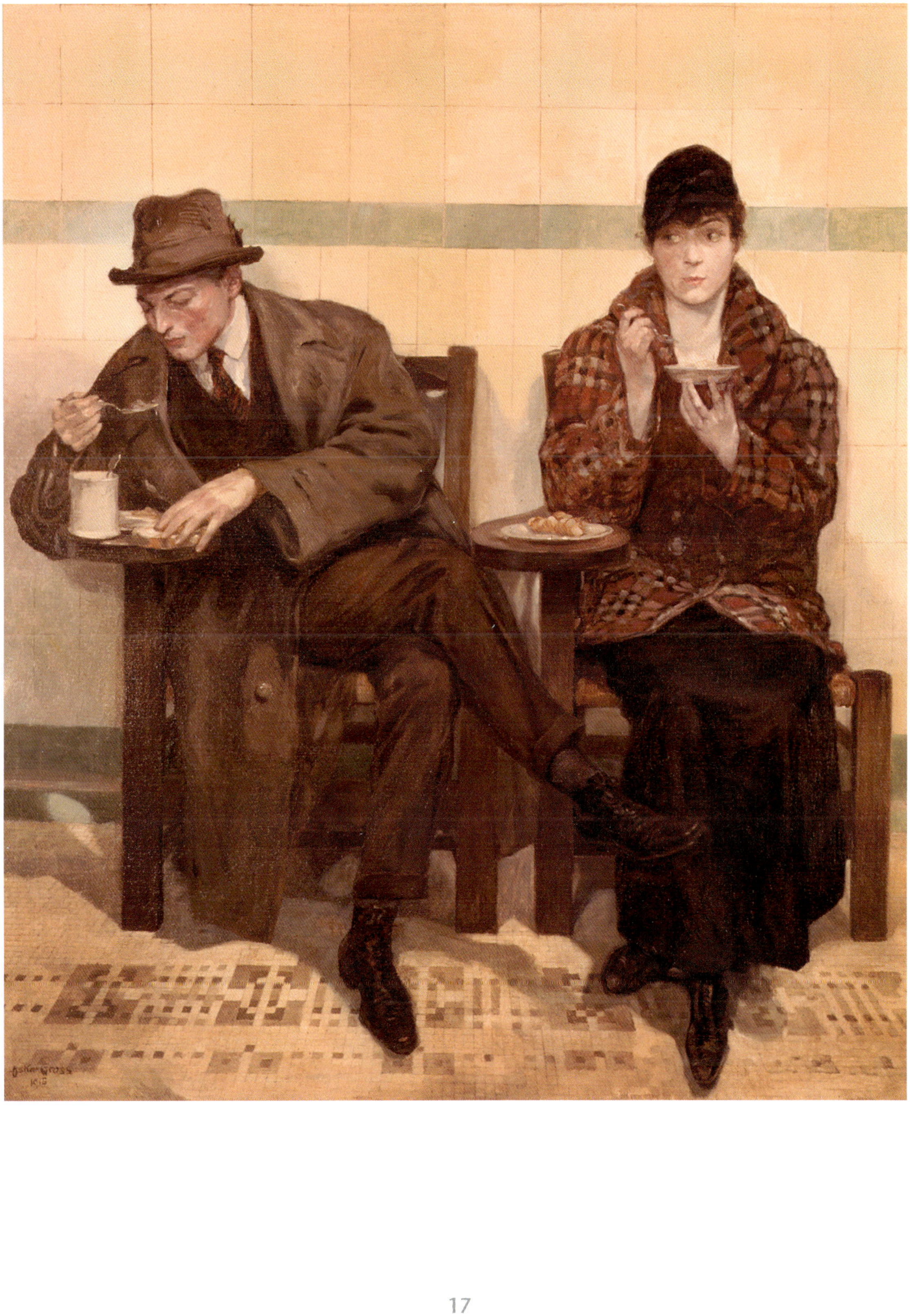

Alfred Eisnstaedt
American, 1898-1995

Untitled (V.J. Day, Times Square)
silver print, 1945
14 x 11 inches
Museum of Fine Arts, St. Petersburg, FL. Purchased with support of National Endowment for the Arts Photography Purchase Grant, 1977, 1981.35

Alfred Eisnstaedt's picture of a random kiss on VJ Day is one of the three or four most-recognized photographs of the Second World War: joyous, triumphant, spontaneous. According to Eisnstaedt, "people tell me that when I am in heaven they will remember this picture." It captures the end of an amazing four years in our history. During that time, millions of Americans who had never left their towns or neighborhoods were sent around the globe, in uniform, with a purpose far greater than their past individual concerns — and the nation was forever changed.

Relationships became less predictable. Couples who in pre-war times would have never met fell suddenly in love: Southern belles at USO clubs dancing with Midwestern sergeants, Radcliffe graduates working at the Pentagon meeting Army aviators from L.A., women at work in factories for the first time falling for sailors on leave. Old restraints loosened, established taboos ("nice girls don't...") disappeared. Eisnstaedt's setting captures that. Everyone looking at the kissing couple is smiling, even the grandmother on the right. Thirty years earlier, in 1915, all the onlookers would have been shaking their heads. Even light and dark seem to have lost their ancient moral symbolism.

The contrasts in the picture — dark sailor and white nurse; couple standing, crowd strolling aimlessly; sailors on the left, civilians on the right, but all smiling — create an overall unity. Eisnstaedt had seen this sailor kissing every woman he encountered, and waited for him to reach the nurse in her white uniform. But his camera captured more than light and dark. The sudden embrace of the couple is almost a swing movement, two dancers swirling in a jitterbug, the dance of the times in which couples at breathtaking speed join, separate, and join again, as vast movements of troops made countless romantic couples do. If not for long, at least for now — and here we have its final joyousness.

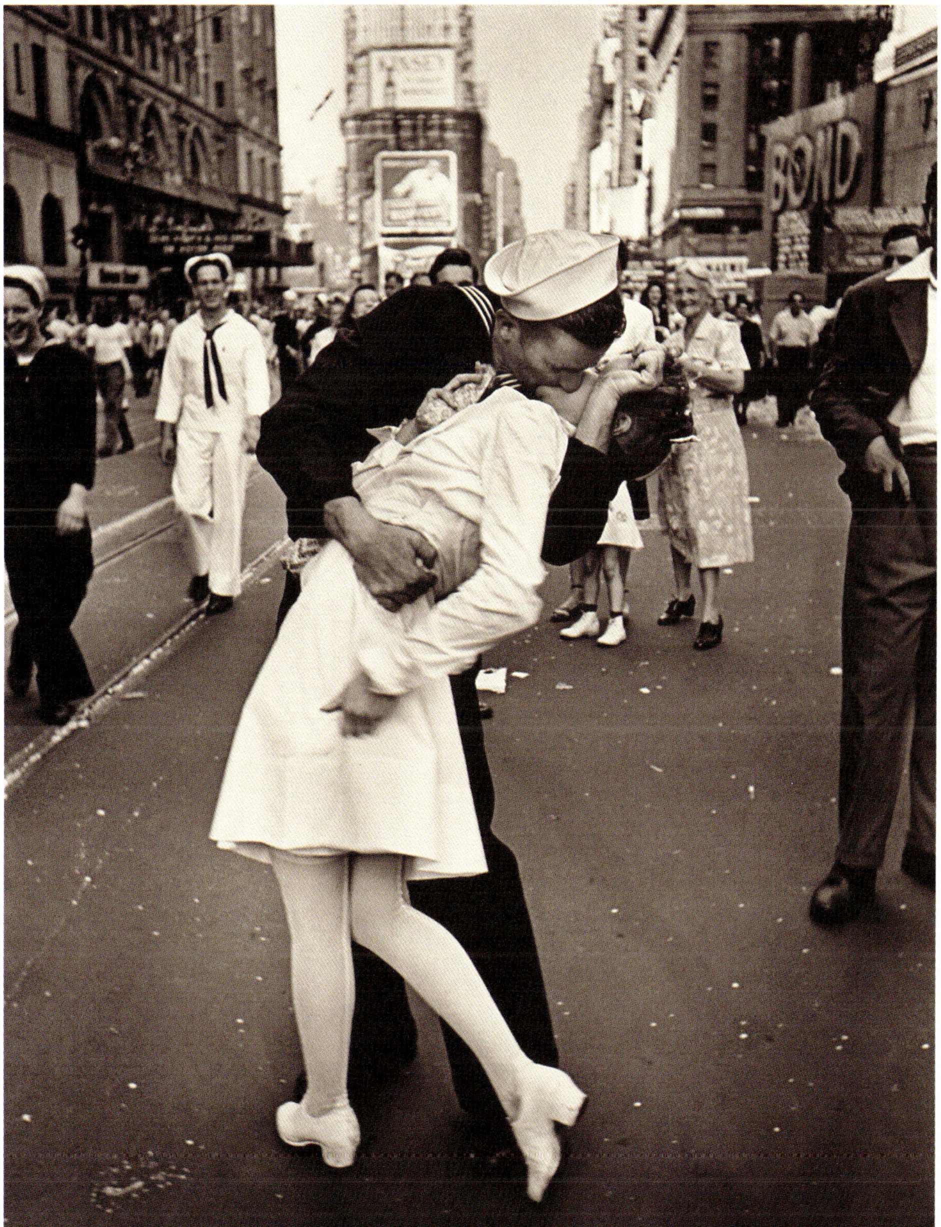
BOND

Howard Pyle
American, 1853-1911

When All the World Was Young
for *Harper's Monthly Magazine,* August 1909
oil on canvas, 1909
36⅝ x 24⅝ inches
Delaware Art Museum, Museum Purchase, 1912.1096

5

For two generations or more, children in love with books have been entranced with the illustrations of Howard Pyle. The words of *Robin Hood* and Mallory's *King Arthur* took a lively shape in many minds through his full-page color renderings. Less well known nowadays are Pyle's magazine illustrations. *When All the World Was Young* appeared in the August 1909 *Harper's Monthly Magazine,* at the peak of the golden age of illustration that ran from roughly 1880 to 1930. Among Pyle's many students are such names as Maxwell Parish and N.C. Wyeth. Eventually, the Depression's collapse of many publications, the Second World War's concern with photographed realities, and finally the 1950's triumph of television, spelled the end of general interest, broadly middle-class publications. But, in their heyday, the illustrators enjoyed wealth and fame.

Certain conventions are observed here as in many other works of this exhibit. The man is clothed in dark colors, the woman in white and shades of pink. Physically, the couple look a bit too perfect: the woman's grace and long neck could come from a Jane Austen adaptation on PBS, the man looks like a combination of halfback and Heathcliff. The blossoming trees are symbols of love's early stages, in which the couple's physical separation seems appropriate. Pyle's fine detail, though, gives these elements a particularity and rich texture.

What is most striking in Pyle's work is its strong narrative sense. Here the couple is not just beginning a courtship ritual as in Garnier's painting, *A Courting Couple* (catalogue no. 6) — Pyle presents drama and conflict, which can only come after the preliminaries are past. The earnest look on the man's face, the woman's apparent but clearly contrived attention to her sewing, hint that a question has just been or will shortly be asked, perhaps even *the* question. But the answer is not a guaranteed yes. These two are still thinking, of joined or separate futures. The brick wall divides the dark green of foliage from the bright pastels of blossoms and sky. The picture focuses on the gate of division, even as it looks through to a possible future of vine-covered cottages and domesticity. There may be a reference to Luke 13:24, "try to enter by the narrow gate, because many will try to enter and will not succeed." This is a defining moment in two lives.

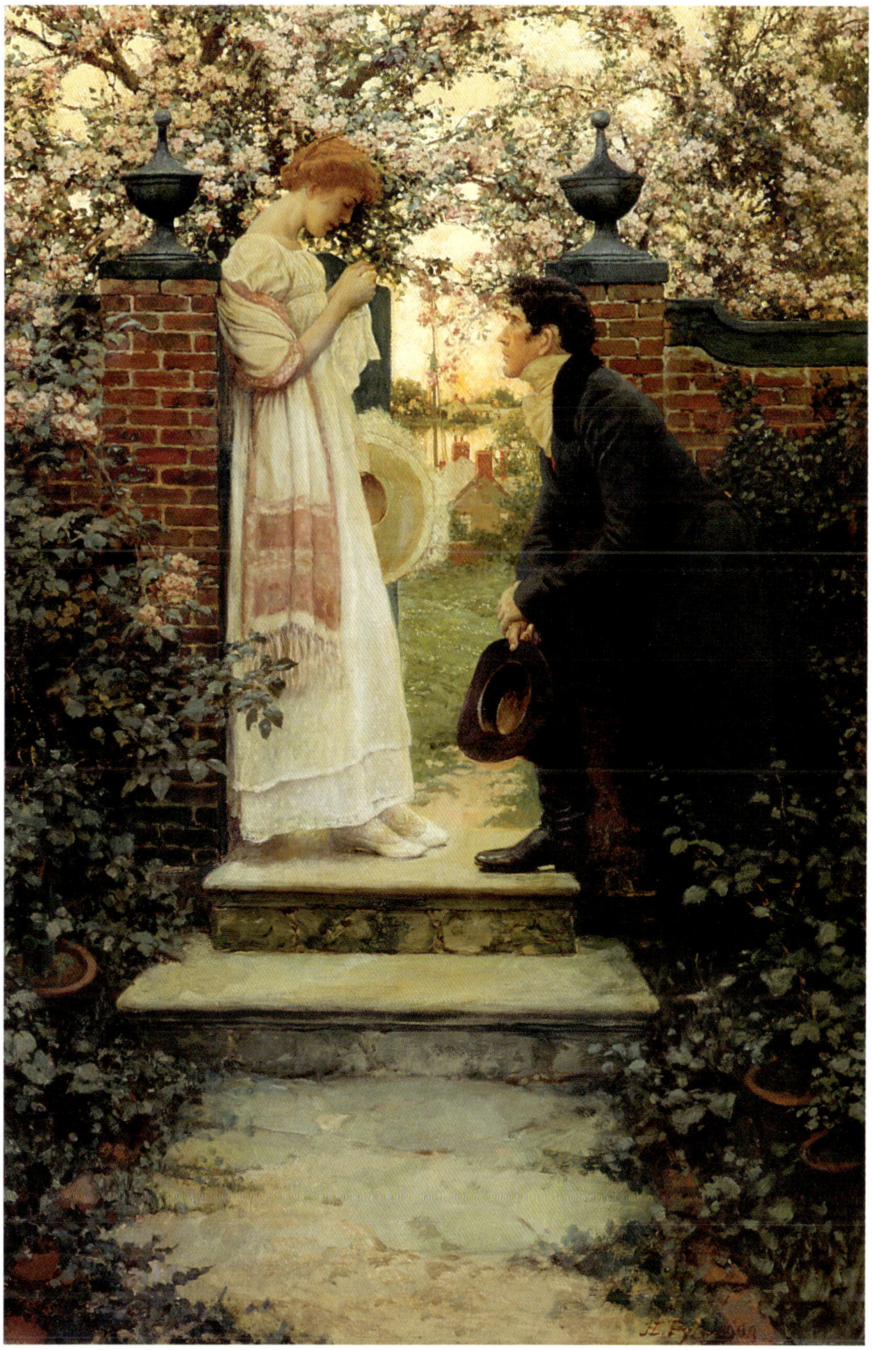

JULES ARSENE GARNIER
FRENCH 1847-1889

A Courting Couple
oil on canvas, 1880
31 x 18⅝ inches
Courtesy of Hammer Galleries, New York, NY

'Courtship' has a formal, stilted ring, coming from a tradition centuries old. The word expresses the life of a court, the crowds of nobles in the retinue of a monarch. These hangers-on lived often by their verbal wits, their ability to flatter diplomatically, and their willingness to amuse, even at the cost of their own self-worth. The spirit of this world was set down in the sixteenth-century Italian *Book of the Courtier* by Baldassare Castiglione. These ideas have reverberated through our culture ever since. Even casual, democratic Americans hunger for the ordered worlds of Emily Post and Miss Manners.

Jules Arsene Garnier's painting of 1880 was intentionally set in a distant past. The couple is dressed in late sixteenth-century costume: he in ruff, hose and canions, she in long dress and farthingale to make her appear tall and graceful. He bows courteously, as she looks up, pleased not to be wasting time on the book she never intended to read. In the days before telephones and computers, most courtships took place, as here, in semi-public spaces, gardens, squares, ballrooms, or parlors. This is the moment just before he speaks, for it is with the speaking of words that courtship, the approach of a courtier, begins. As the courtier adores his lord, the lover worships, with Petrarchan focus, his beloved. Words of courtship have to be measured and uttered with care — many a teenaged boy learns for the first time, in talking with a girl, that an unintended word can hurt, can even bring on tears. ("I didn't, like, mean that.") Spoken words create intimacy. Words written in love-letters may last for years; they may become part of history or lawsuits. But spoken words are only for the hearer and only for the moment. In the very public life of a court (or a modern high school), these wisps of private conversations may be the only chance for a couple to differentiate themselves from the crowd.

Where will this beginning end? Marriage? Heartbreak? Joy? Garnier gives no hint. It is late spring or early summer; but beyond that, the green background provides only a generic timelessness. It is the pattern, renewed again, that matters: the formulaic that may lead to the intensely private.

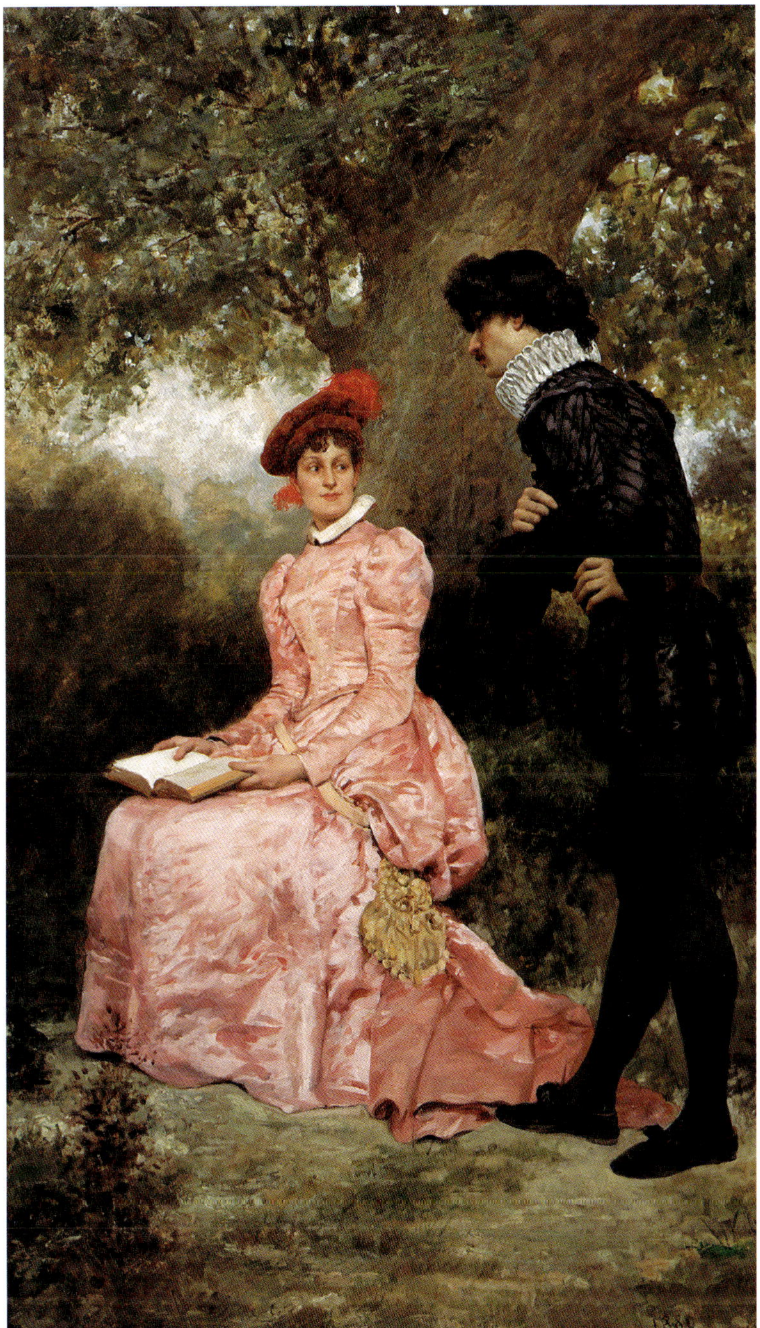

Attributed to Filippo Angeli called
Filippo Napoletano
Neapolitan, c. 1600-1640

Saint George Liberating the Princess
oil on canvas, c. 1625
51½ x 38 inches
Frances Lehman Loeb Art Center, Vassar College, Poughkeepsie, NY, gift of Mr. and Mrs. R. Kirk Askew, Jr., 1966.22

7

A moral code for feudal chivalry and the ideals of 'courtly love' developed in the twelfth century, first in the troubadour courts of Southern France and somewhat later in castles in Northern France. In this ideal of behavior, a knight sworn in political fealty to a sovereign lord would take a similar pledge to some distant and unattainable love, his lady. Although courtly love was more a literary than a social institution, people being what they are, the characters often turned a secret worship from afar into physical closeness. Lancelot and Guinevere, Tristan and Isolde (physical lovers) are still, after centuries, famous as adulterers. Rudel de Blaye and his unseen love, the Countess of Tripoli, are but a literary footnote. Surprisingly, these ideas are still current. In films and novels, poor but honest boys fall in love with high-class girls, "worlds above them," and eventually earn that love with some great deed, like winning the big game or saving the life of a small animal. We still talk of 'courting' and 'Prince Charming' and a 'search for love' and 'winning someone's heart.' Andreas Capellanus, the twelfth-century author of a treatise on love, says, "Honesty of character gains a love." Hollywood seconds the motion every chance it gets.

In the same century, knights returning from the Crusades brought back to Western Europe the Eastern cult of St. George. Little historical information exists about this Roman tribune and martyr; but the tale of a soldier passing by when a young maiden was about to be sacrificed to a dragon triggered a strong response in these young barons. St. George became the patron of England, whose national flag still carries the cross that was once the crusaders' standard. He is usually portrayed in the "armor of God" (Ephesians 6:11) like the Archangel Michael, slaying the dragon symbolic of the devil (Revelations 12:7-9). Here, a later moment in the tale is portrayed by Filippo Napoletano. The man in dark armor is mounted; the woman stands, dressed in rich and colorful fabric. The saved maiden and brave knight look on each other's face for the first time. Her look is one of devotion; his is a frank appraisal. He has already performed his great deed; her response is an adoring look of hero worship. According to the *Golden Legend,* St. George never fell in love with the girl; he rode on to Palestine and martyrdom under the emperor Diocletian. Napoletano's St. George looks as if he has the same intent.

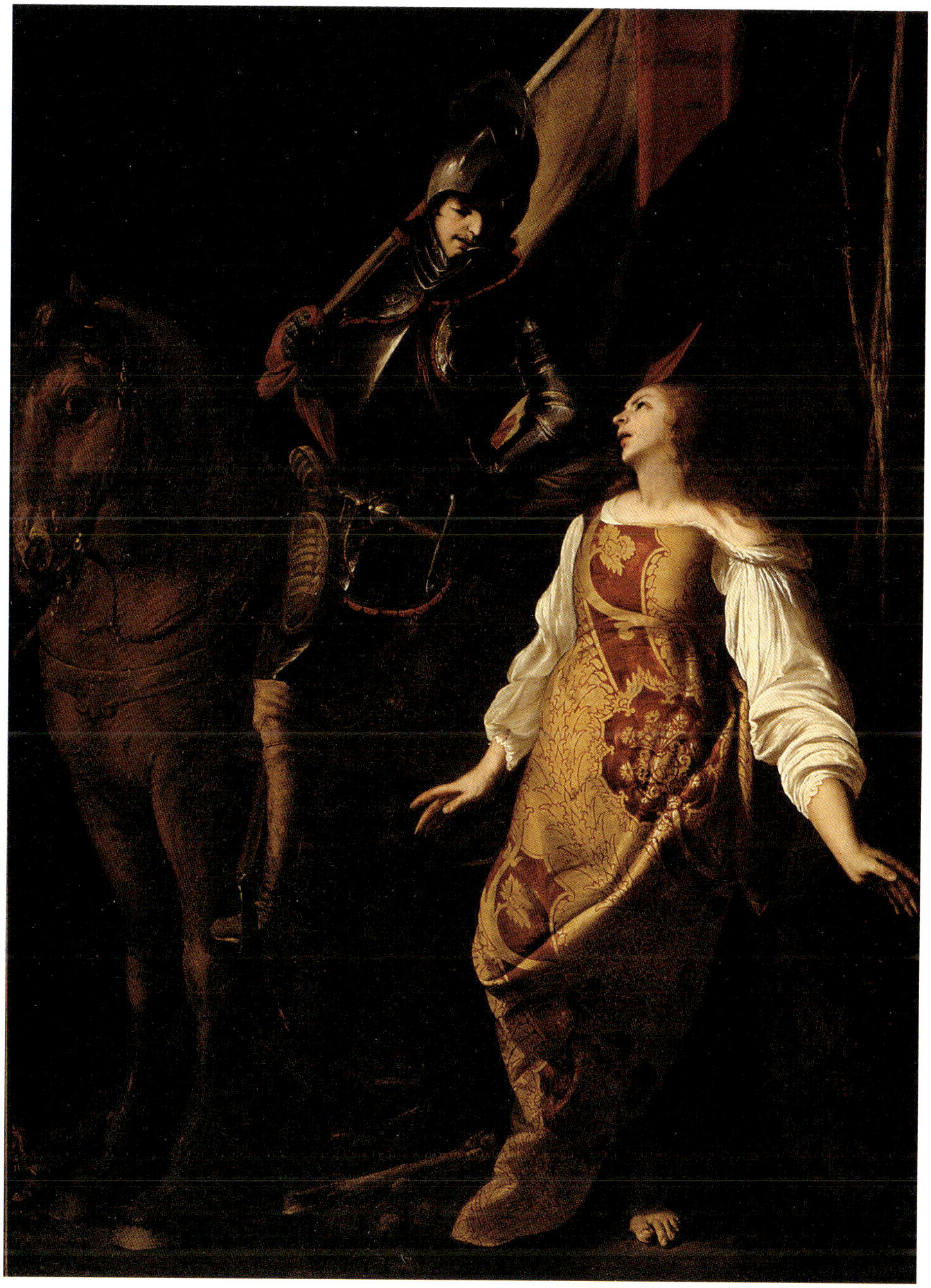

Jean-Auguste-Dominique Ingres
French, 1780-1867

Perseus and Andromeda
oil on canvas, c. 1819
7¾ x 6⅜ inches
The Detroit Institute of Arts, Bequest of Robert H. Tannahill, 70.170

Ovid in his *Metamorphoses* IV:610-764, tells the story of the rescue of the beautiful young princess, Andromeda, by the hero, Perseus, conqueror of Medusa. It became a favorite theme for both Roman wall paintings and Renaissance artists. Andromeda's mother had often praised her daughter's beauty, so excessively that the Nereids, nymphs of the waves, were insulted and complained to Neptune. The sea-god sent a monster to ravage the coast of Ethiopia, Andromeda's home; and to appease him, the king had ordered her bound to a rock on the shore, as a sacrifice. Perseus was flying overhead in his winged sandals. The young man was struck by her beauty, so perfect he first thought her a statue carved from marble, and fell instantly in love. But at that moment the sea monster emerged and Perseus had to win her hand by slaying the beast. A marriage feast followed before the sun set.

For Ingres, it is the girl, not the hero, who is the central figure. She is completely modest, even in her nudity. Ovid says she would have hidden her face with her hands had they not been chained. She stands separated by the rock from the frenzied combat. Ingres painted several versions of a similar scene — beautiful nude lashed to the rocks, sea serpent, unknown hero — called "Roger Delivering Angelica" which comes from a Perseus-like tale in Ariosto's *Orlando Furioso* X:92-112. The most famous of these, the 1819 version, hangs in the Louvre.

This tale of an abandoned beauty saved by a mysterious stranger has had strong psychological appeal for two millennia. Think of a teen-aged girl, told by her mother she is pretty, but disbelieving the words. Feeling misunderstood, alienated from her family, she hopes for rescue by the tall, dark, clichéd stranger of Harlequin romance novels. The monster comes ever closer — it might represent exclusive school cliques or her own hesitant sexual awareness or the loneliness unique to each teenager but common to all. Such agonies of the growing soul and such hopes for rescue explain the willingness to endure college mixers in the '50s and singles' bars in the '90s. A millennium hence, there will still be settings in which a young girl will feel herself stared at by the crowd and will hope to be saved by a special hero; and there will be some artist ready to freeze the moment of rescue through art.

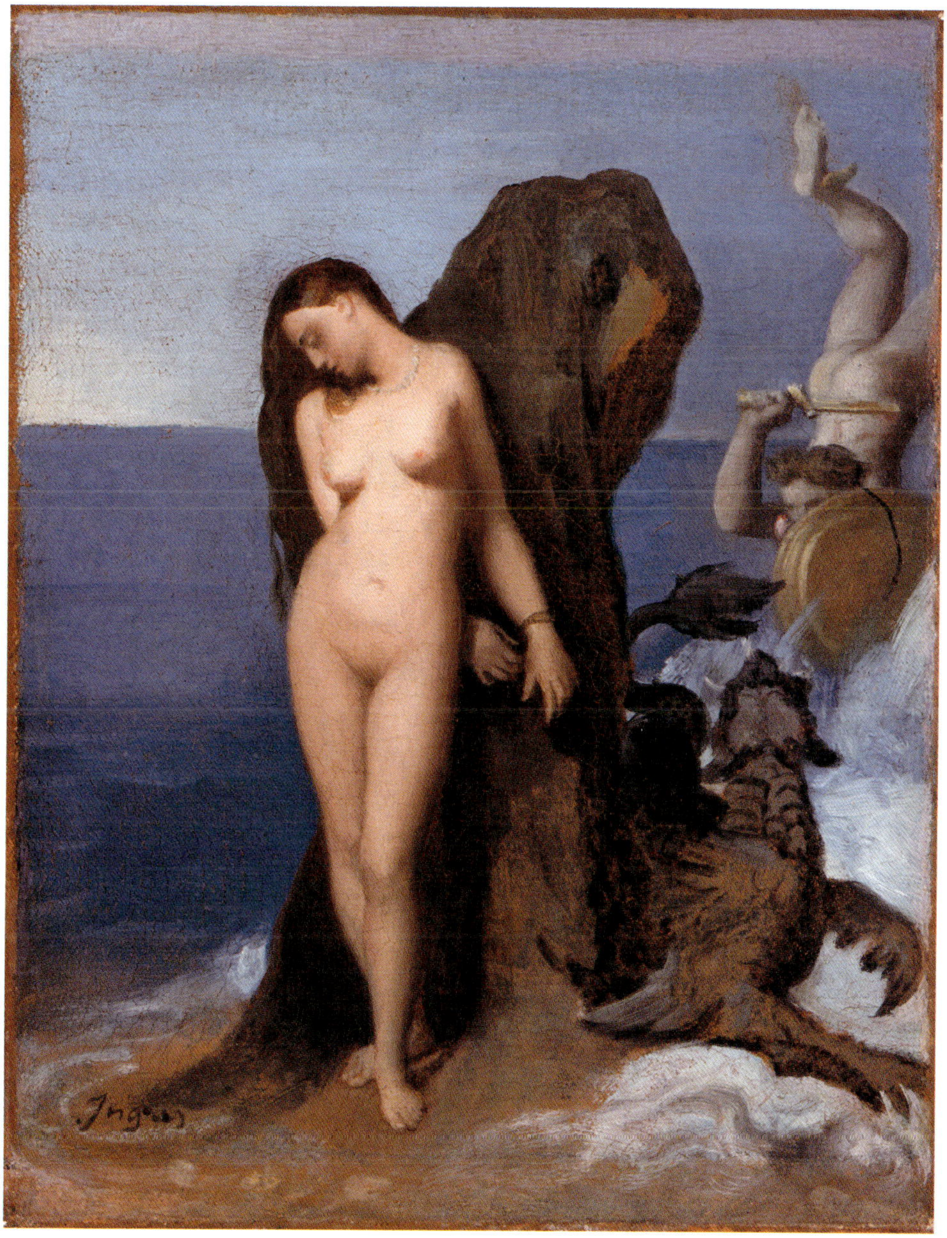

Gaspare Traversi

Italian, c. 1722-1770

The Detected Love Letter
oil on canvas, c. 1760
32½ x 42¾ inches
Bequest of John Ringling, 1936
Collection of The John and Mable Ringling Museum of Art, the State Art Museum of Florida, SN170

Active in Naples and Rome in the mid-eighteenth century, Gaspare Traversi was a painter of religious and comic genre subjects. His was the world of Casanova and *liaisons dangereuses* and *Così fan tutte:* a society in which the privileged enjoyed the easy, cultured life of the *ancien régime.* Such a social setting afforded countless opportunities for parties, intrigues, tête-à-têtes, all bound together by letters. In our world of e-mail, cellphones and faxes, we tend to forget how much information a letter-writer had to include in this infrequent means of communication, and how dangerous it might have been to have these secret details known. A misdirected letter or a bribed servant could set off a drawing-room explosion.

Such a servant may be laughing in the upper-right hand corner of the painting, but the family is in an uproar. The father and mother, clearly aging with thin, angular faces and high, receding hairlines, berate their daughter, whose more rounded face and figure indicate her age as mid-twenties. Their hands are clenched. He clutches the letter and probably shouts about family dishonor, while the mother just wails. The daughter's daintily held handkerchief, however, looks like an actress' gesture — has this scene been played before? Such a possibility would have occurred to, and amused, the worldly, aristocratic purchasers of such a painting. They, too, well knew that the path of love is never smooth.

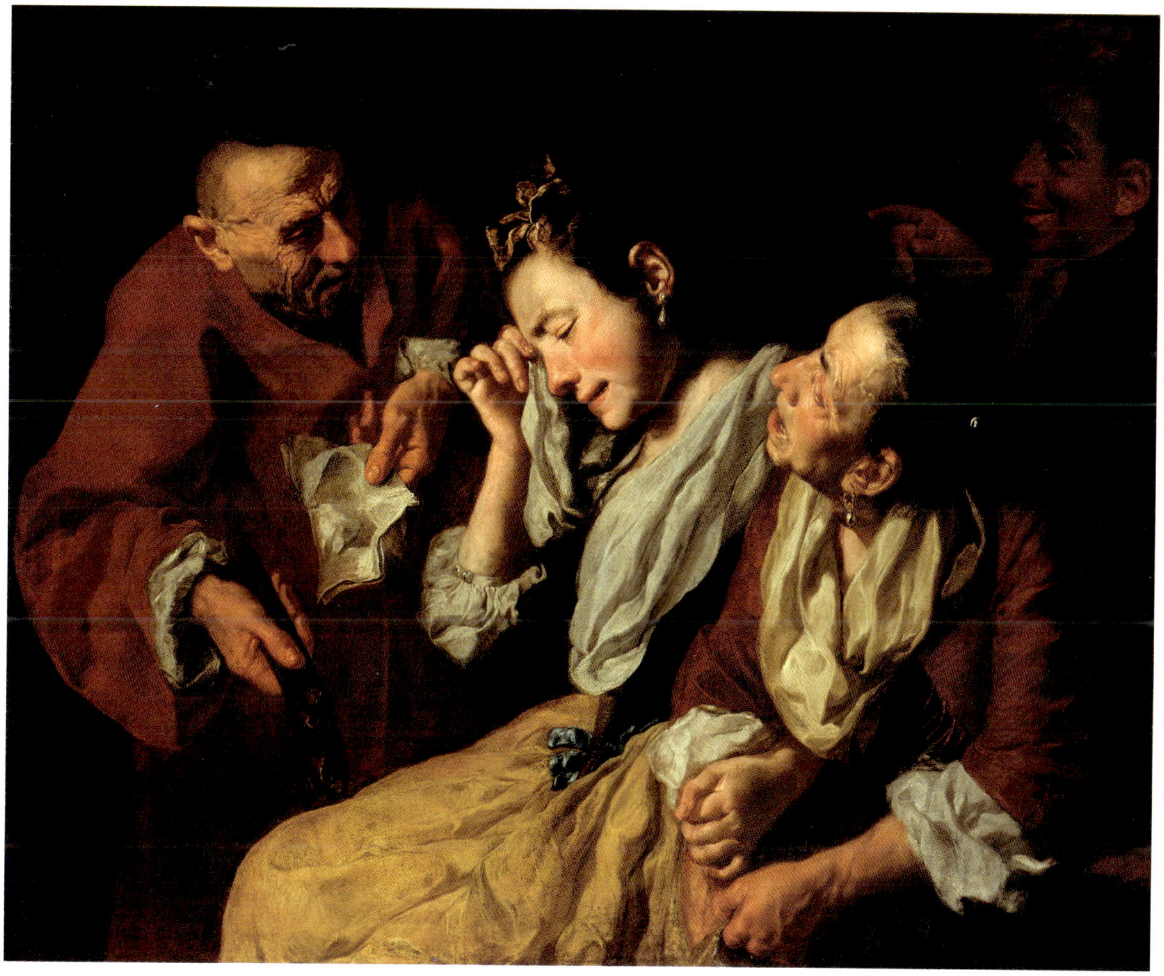

Edwin Longsden Long

British, 1829-1891

Love's Labour Lost
oil on canvas, 1885
50 x 75¼ inches
Dahesh Museum, New York, 1995.10

Shakespeare's play of nearly the same title tells how four young men renounce all worldly delights, in particular the company of women, to devote themselves to study. By Act V, naturally, they have abandoned their philosophical pursuits and fallen deeply in love. Shakespeare's academic romp shares only a title with this painting — the play's tone and ending move in a different direction.

In this pre-Raphaelite, faux-Egyptian oil, an astonishing wealth of detail is presented to comment on and focus attention toward the unidentified noble young woman. By slightly changing the play's title, Edwin Long makes 'lost' a past participle, an event over and done. That is the look on the princess' face. She stares sadly into the distance as her attendants despair of interesting her in child-like or courtly play. At the lower left lie forgotten toys, and music too has lost its charm. One servant has danced herself into exhaustion, in vain.

The artist displaces the young woman from her 'natural' position in the center of the painting where her head would be directly under the papyrus clump, a symbol of life and young joy, in the fresco on the back wall. To her left but cowering into the far corner of the wall is a pet monkey, possibly symbolic of the god Toth, god of writing and measurement. Did a letter go astray? To her right stands a sad-eyed animal, the symbol of the god Seth, who represents the forces of confusion in the world. Her thought is elsewhere, and as the title and her sad look suggest, she has moved beyond vague stirrings and is able to know a love, now lost.

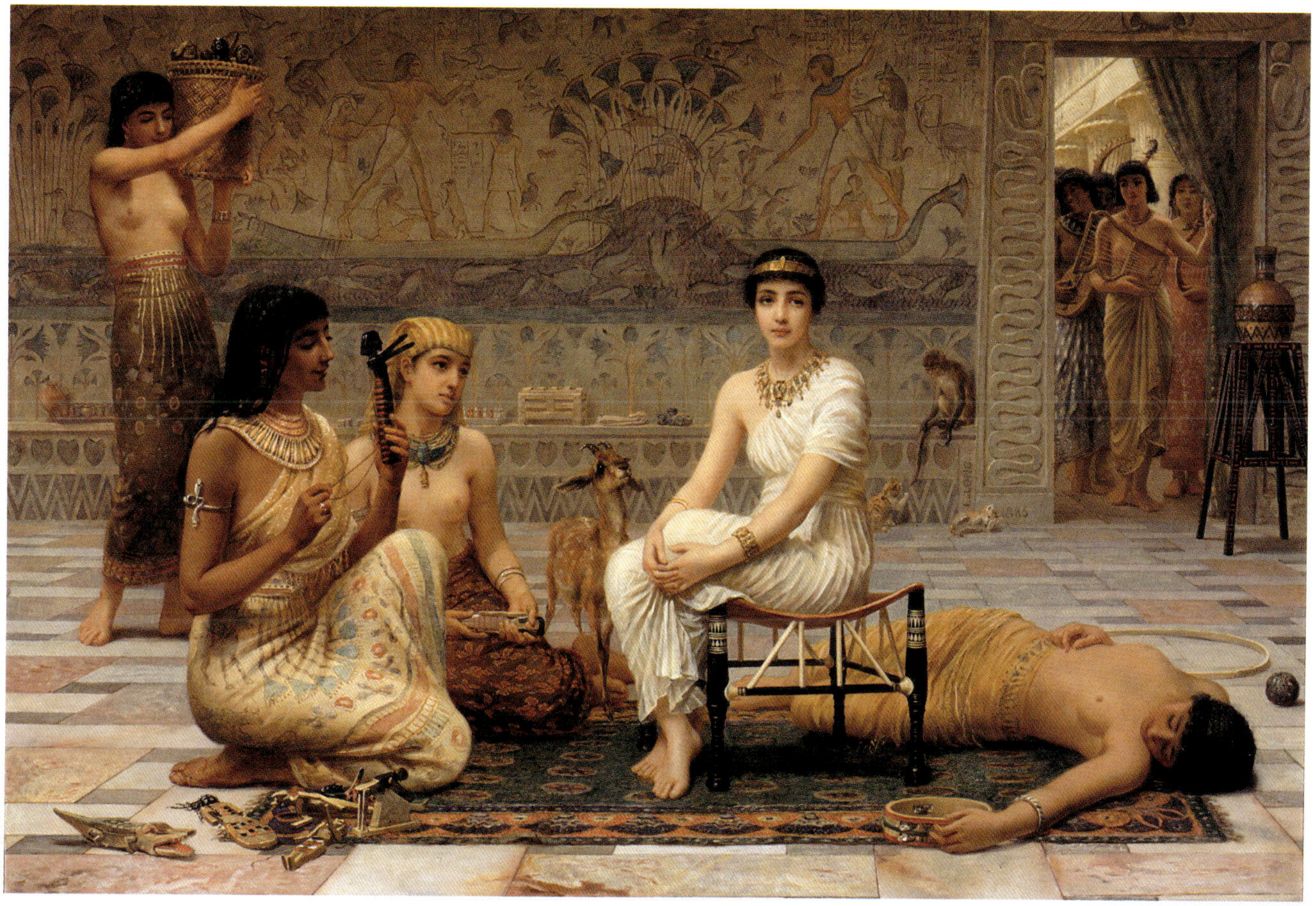

Niccolo dell'Abate
Italian, c. 1509-1571

Eros and Psyche
oil on canvas, c. 1560
39¼ x 36½ inches
The Detroit Institute of Arts, Founders Society Purchase, Robert H. Tannahill Foundation Fund, 65.347

In the second century A.D., Latin writer Apuleius tells the story of this pair (*Metamorphoses* IV:28 — VI: 24), a charming fairytale of his own construction and not a part of classical mythology. Psyche, the youngest of three princesses, is the most beautiful of girls, and some say her beauty surpasses even that of Venus. The goddess of love, enraged by such a challenge, sends her young son, Eros, to punish her challenger. We know Eros more commonly as Cupid, but both the Greek and Latin names mean 'desire'. The young winged god, however, falls in love with the beautiful mortal and contrives to wed her. To maintain secrecy he comes to her only in darkness, and she is forbidden to look upon him. (The sculpture, *Cupid and Psyche,* catalogue no. 12, shows the moment of her discovery of his identity.) To punish her betrayal of his request for secrecy, he flees; and the girl is pursued by Venus, who seizes her, beats her and sets several impossible tasks for her. But soon enough true love triumphs. At Eros' request, Jupiter, father of the gods, approves of the marriage and grants Psyche immortality and divine status. The child she has been carrying is born and named Voluptas (Pleasure).

We are used to thinking of Cupid as a mere boy, but artists and writers in classical times portrayed him at various ages, from three to seventeen. Dell'Abbate's painting shows a teen-aged pair at the end of the story, ensconced on Mount Olympus, at rest in the delights of their marriage bed. (Earlier bedroom scenes of the two in Apuleius are charming, but are set in total darkness, not the friendliest of painterly settings.) The crumpled bedclothes hint just how delightful the night has been so far. The young god's bow and quiver of arrows, the weapons he uses to bring love's joy and heartbreak to mankind, sit idly at the side. Husband and wife, they now talk, in agreement as their heads incline toward each other. Reddish hues highlight the god who sends out the fire of love. Psyche's flesh is more the fine white of marble.

Longing and the Soul (Psyche is Greek for 'soul') — it is tempting to read the tale as a Platonic myth with deep psychological insight. The girl is open, good-hearted, impressionable ('very simple' says Apuleius), a *tabula rasa.* Longing causes her to desert home and family for an unknown life, part charming and part threatening. Once parted from the object of desire, the soul wanders throughout the world and is willing to undergo suffering and challenges until it is reunited. Dell'Abbate, an Italian painter for the French king at Fontainebleau, may have started with that intention, but he is distracted by the sheer delight of telling of love's triumph. Apuleius' *bella fabula* (pretty tale) ends, like most of Shakespeare's comedies, with a wedding banquet, a lively feast that points to the night ahead.

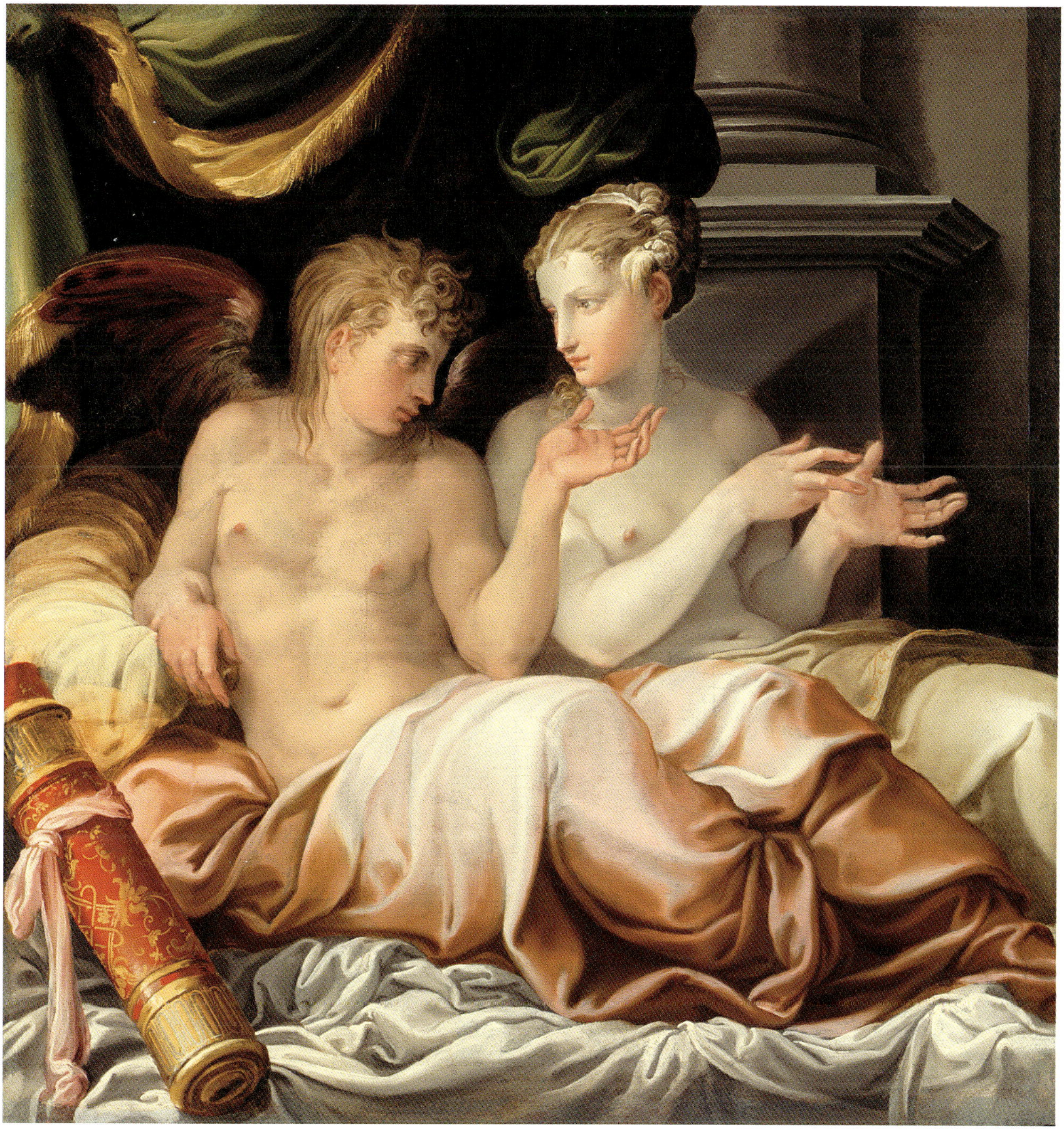

GIOVANNI BATTISTA FOGGINI
ITALIAN, 1652-1725

Cupid and Psyche
bronze, c. 1700
13⅜ x 14⅝ x 9¼ inches
The Detroit Institute of Arts, Founders Society Purchase, Robert H. Tannahill Foundation Fund, 81.695

This charming eighteenth-century bronze captures the scene portrayed in Apuleius' *Metamorphoses* V:22-24. The gentle Psyche, with a beauty rivaling that of Cupid's mother, has married an unknown, invisible husband who visits her only at night. At the prompting of her two evil older sisters, (a family arrangement that has produced stories from *Cinderella* to *King Lear*) she has hidden an oil lamp under her bed to see for the first time her lover and to slay him if he proves to be the horrendous monster her sisters have imagined. Against Cupid's strict commands, the girl rises from their bed and holds the lamp, strikingly, as far from Cupid's face as the space of the sculpture allows. This is the moment of discovery, as she pulls back the sheet and is stunned to see, instead of the expected "monstrous snake ... its bloody neck oozing noxious poisons," a vision of beauty:

> *On his golden head she saw the glorious hair drenched with ambrosia; wandering over his milk-white neck and rosy cheeks were the neat tangle of his curls. ... Along his shoulders, white feathers glistened like flowers in the morning dew; and although his wings were at rest, soft and delicate little plumes along their edges quivered restlessly in wanton play.*

From this moment comes near disaster. This is a moment of universal significance, the shock when the lover is seen as he or she really is, one of the true tests of a relationship. A drop of oil from the lamp will fall on the god's shoulder, waking and wounding him. Betrayed, he will take flight as his pregnant wife grasps his legs; but she will be forced to drop to earth, exhausted and in deep distress. Their charming interlude shattered, her immediate course will be to wander the world, seeking her lost Cupid and hiding from the jealous rage of his mother, Venus. The dynamism of this late Baroque piece indicates the disturbances ahead. The deeply cut, almost frenzied lines of the bed-linen on which the lovers have been resting have the look of waves in a storm at sea. The long curve of Psyche's right arm, pulling back the sheet, shields the pregnancy their love has made, the pregnancy that infuriates Venus, according to Apuleius, clearly a middle-aged goddess of love (V:30-31):

> *Cupid, you worthless, unlovable seducer, you presume that only you are of noble birth and that I am too old to conceive. Well, know that I will produce another son much better than you. Now that marriage of yours will taste sour and bitter.*

Through a tale of gods and goddesses, *Cupid and Psyche* tell us much of the emotions of humans in love and love as a process of human recognition.

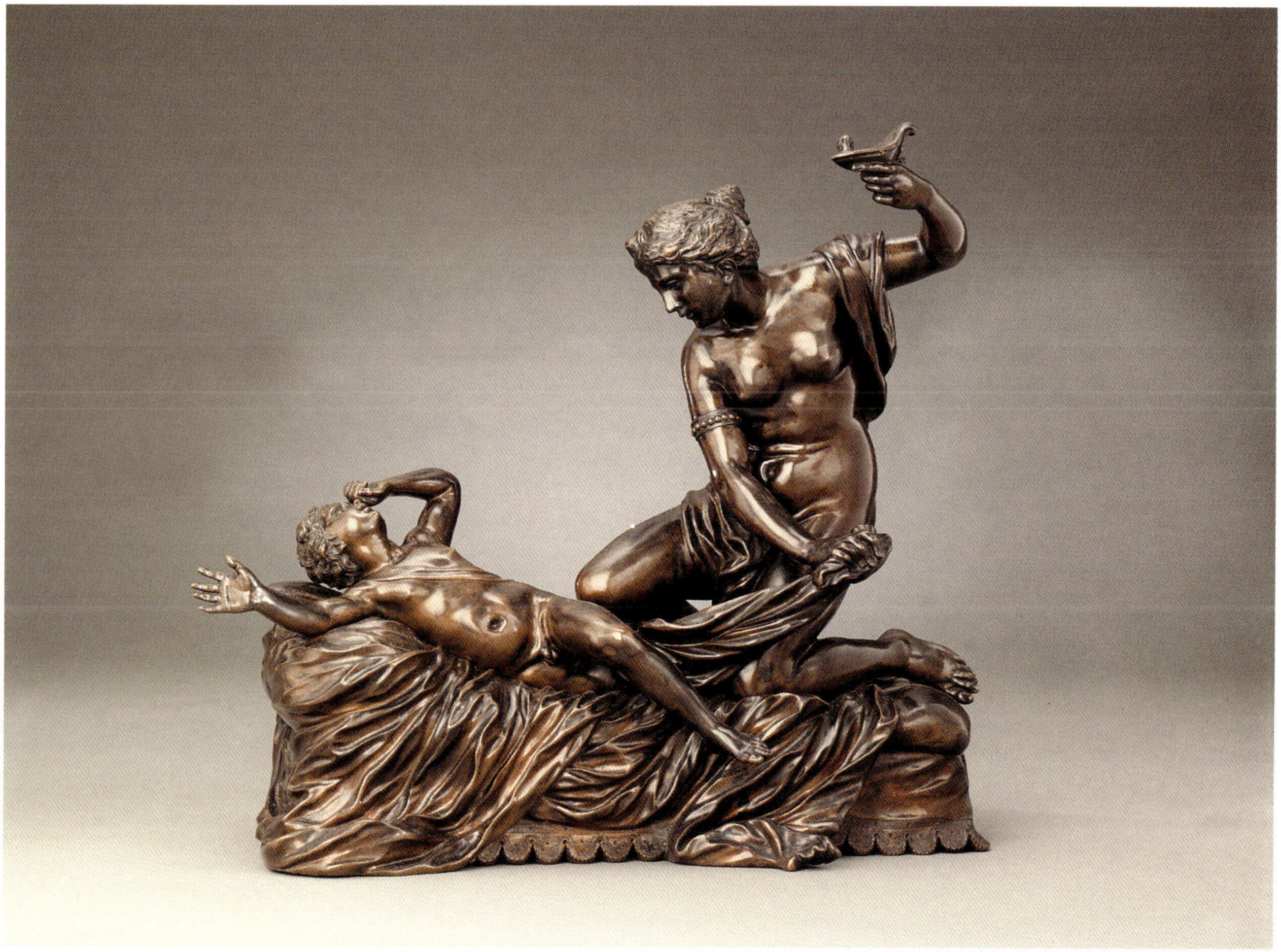

Benjamin West
American, 1738-1820

Romeo and Juliet
oil on canvas, 1778
50 x 44¼ inches
New Orleans Museum of Art: Museum purchase, Women's Volunteer Committee Fund, 73.33

In Act III, scene 5 of Shakespeare's *Romeo and Juliet,* the two lovers stand, at daybreak, by Juliet's window.

> Juliet. ... *O, now be gone; more light and light it grows.*
>
> Romeo. *More light and light; more dark and dark our woes.*
>
> Enter Nurse, to the chamber.
>
> Nurse. *Madam!*
>
> Juliet. *Nurse?*
>
> Nurse. *Your lady mother is coming to the chamber: The day is broke; be wary, look about.*

The poetic song to the dawn of the playfully ironic lovers — "It was the nightingale" "It was the lark" — is interrupted by the prose of Juliet's nurse. In Benjamin West's painting of the scene, the pair are framed by the light of the window, the nurse by the shadowed background of the room. The lovers' heads are bare but joined together, the nurse's is veiled as she looks backward at the danger of possible discovery. Their self-absorption pays no attention to her; and the tragedy will soon show that they disregard her practical advice to be wary.

Benjamin West was, in late eighteenth-century England, one of the first American painters to establish a formidable reputation for himself back in the mother country. He was also one of the first painters to appreciate the dramatic visual possibilities in scenes from Shakespeare's plays. Here, if one excludes the tense drama created by the figure of the nurse, he shows two lovers in the early, clinging stage of closeness. Before this point, there had been the even earlier stage of the delight in mutual discovery: "O, it is my love! O that she knew she were!" Romeo had said earlier, in the balcony scene. Now that stage has progressed into a desperate desire to hold each other. Departure might mean disappearance: "Thinkst thou we shall ever meet again?" asks Juliet later in this scene. A world, a city, a room shrink to the narrow circumference of an embrace.

But love is never so purely bipolar as lovers hope. A marriage unites a bride and groom, but it can divide two families. Romeo had begun the play swooning over the "fair Rosaline": one love chosen means another excluded, often with violent consequences. Or, as here, the silly face-saving feuding of teenage boys launches a chaotic politics in which true love can end only in tragic death. For West, the nurse is the harbinger of that tragedy.

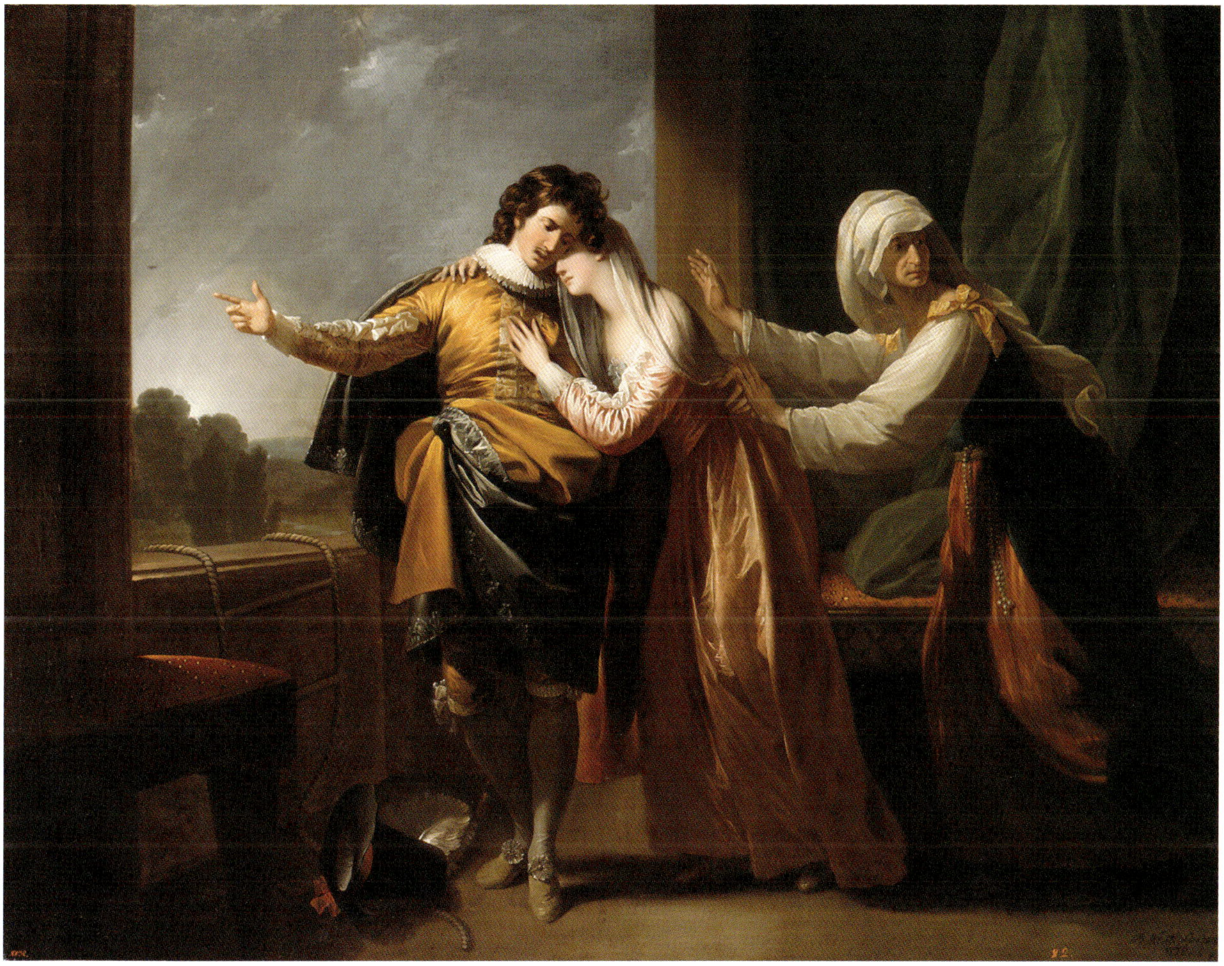

JEAN-AUGUSTE-DOMINIQUE INGRES
FRENCH, 1780-1867

Paolo and Francesca
oil on canvas, c. 1855-60
11½ x 8¾ inches
The Hyde Collection Art Museum, Glen Falls, New York, 1971.24

In Canto V of Dante's *Inferno,* the pilgrim discovers, in the second circle of Hell, two of the souls of the lustful, Paolo and Francesca. At his bidding, the noble wife of the ruler of Rimini tells of the moment of falling in love with the ruler's brother, Paolo. They had been reading a medieval Arthurian romance and had reached the passage where Lancelot and Guinevere share their first adulterous kiss.

... For when we read
how her fond smile was kissed by such a lover
he who is one with me alive and dead
breathed on my lips the tremor of his kiss.

Dante ends with the stunning simplicity of the line "That day we read no further." *(Quel giorno piú non vi legemmo avante.)*

Ingres' painting focuses on that moment. He painted at least six other versions of this tale, but other versions show such elements as their discovery by her husband, Giancotto Malatesta da Rimini. Enraged, he immediately slew them both and was condemned by Dante to the fifth circle of Hell. Here, the sight is of love, not its consequences. The figure of Francesca dominates: her red dress fills a third of the surface. Paolo, who in Dante's rendering is silent, is here, too, almost an afterthought, a thin slice of blue and yellow on the side. The picture's structure is triangular, appropriately for this ménage á trois: the lovers' bodies form a giant triangle, the arms and heads a second smaller one, and the flesh of necks, faces and Paolo's almost disembodied hand a third and even smaller one. The book, a medieval forerunner of Harlequin, falls out of her hand in a triangle echoed by the triangular reading stand to the right. For Dante the event is a tribute to the power and temptation of literature, for Ingres it is the triumph of the flesh, a favorite theme. Although Ingres is noted in many other paintings (such as his *Turkish Bath*) for an embarrassment of carnal riches, he is more powerful when restrained, as here.

Ingres also gives us psychological insight into the moment of becoming aware of love - forbidden love. He uses the oval, mirror-shape he favored for a number of other works. Here, it almost seems a keyhole through which we are peeping in on the pair. Paolo is advancing, focused on Francesca, whereas she is more ambivalent, allowing passivity and apparent hesitancy as a salve to her conscience. She looks down and away, perhaps glancing back at the book, but with a faint smile. The bits of white blouse emerging from her slittered sleeve hint confusion and uncertainty. But the book has been dropped, and the decision has been made. *Quel giorno piú non vi legemmo avante.*

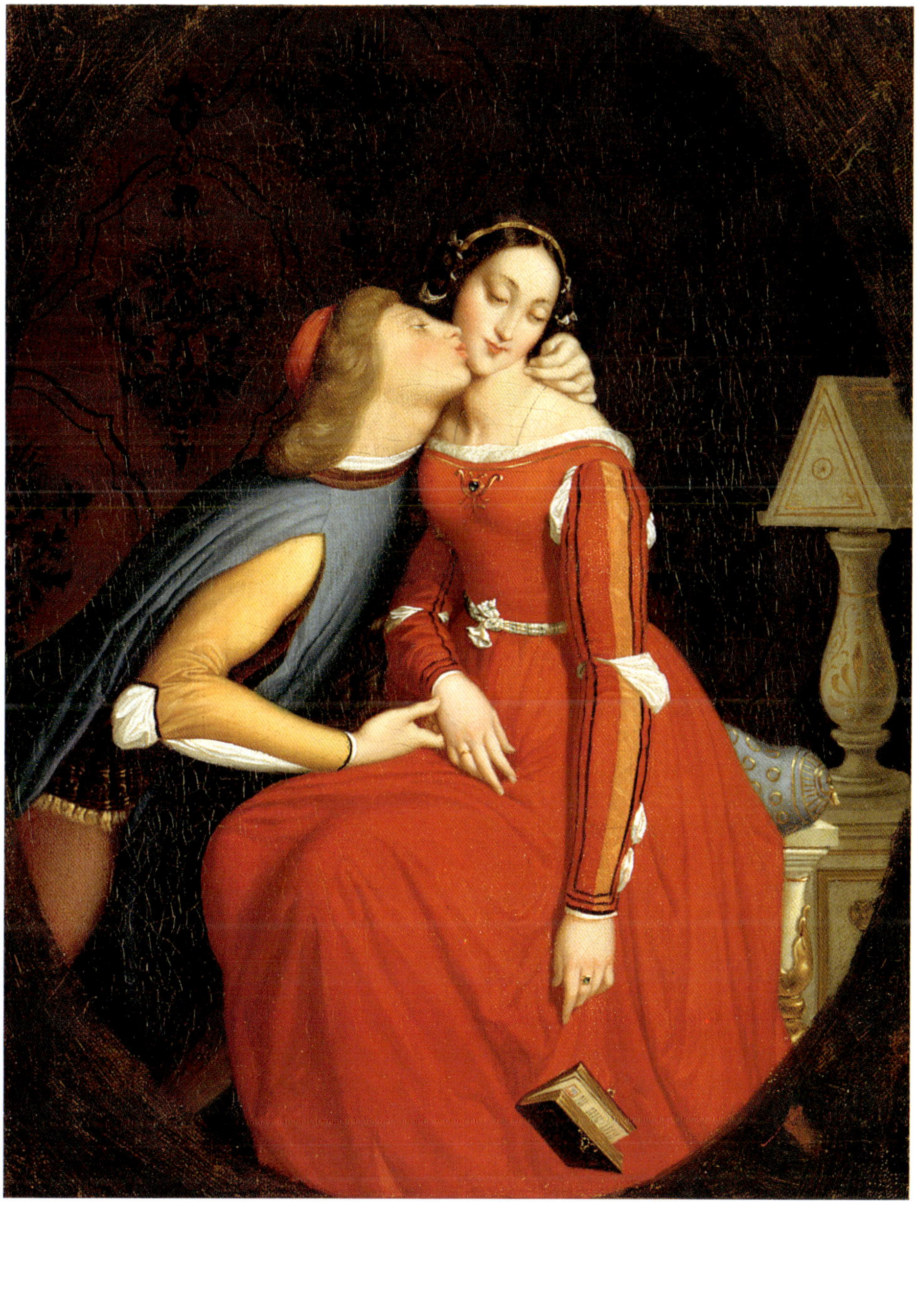

Designed by

Simon Vouet

French, 1590-1649

Rinaldo Prevents the Suicide of the Despairing Armida
wool and silk, seventeenth century
14' 8" x 10' 4"
Flint Institute of Arts, Gift of Viola E. Bray, FBE1961.10

15

In a gallery adjoining this exhibition hangs a cycle of ten Gobelin tapestries, woven in Paris in the second quarter of the seventeenth century and based on designs by Simon Vouet, court painter to Louis XIII. They tell the story of the love, loss and reuniting of Rinaldo and Armida, key characters in Torquato Tasso's sixteenth-century Italian epic poem, *Gerusalemme Liberata*. For this exhibition, the final tapestry has been featured: the triumph of love under adversity.

Like Romeo and Juliet, they seemed star-crossed lovers: Rinaldo the bravest of Christian crusaders besieging Jerusalem and Armida a beautiful, blonde sorceress sent by the Muslim enemies to lure away their leaders. By deceit, she had taken Rinaldo to her enchanted island palace where instead of slaying him she fell suddenly in love (panel 1). "There in an unending April her lover spent with her a time of soft loving" (*Gerusalemme Liberata,* XIV: 71). But his companions followed him to the island, awakened him by a magic diamond shield to a recognition of his duty, and led him back to the Christian camp (panels 4-6). Love's spell broken, Armida vowed vengeance — *vendetta* in the superbly expressive Italian (panels 7 and 8). In the final decisive battle, the Christians are everywhere triumphant; and Armida, in despair, flees. Panel 9 shows her galloping away pursued by an unarmed Cupid, symbol of unrequited love. "Terrified of slavery, she hates her life, despairs of victory or having her revenge" (XX: 117).

Political enemies who fall in love often reach a tragic end; but the tenth tapestry shows a happy outcome. On Rinaldo's side of the design are the strength and vitality of trees and foliage; on Armida's, mostly bare sky and one stripped trunk; but her body leans back onto Rinaldo's. The battle over, he grasps her arm, saving her from death by her own hand. His armored body surrounds and supports her; his strong arms both protect her and arouse her to love. As Armida stares up in unexpected awe, she is about to pledge devotion: "here is your handmaiden; treat her as your heart bids, and let your hint become her law" (XX: 136). The flying Cupid now carries the palm of victory — all the Cupids are Vouet's additions to the story.

In a love story interwoven with potions and deceptions, enchanted islands and magic shields, this last tapestry shows that in the moment of greatest stress love's more natural power overwhelms the politics of opposition and the hopelessness of loss.

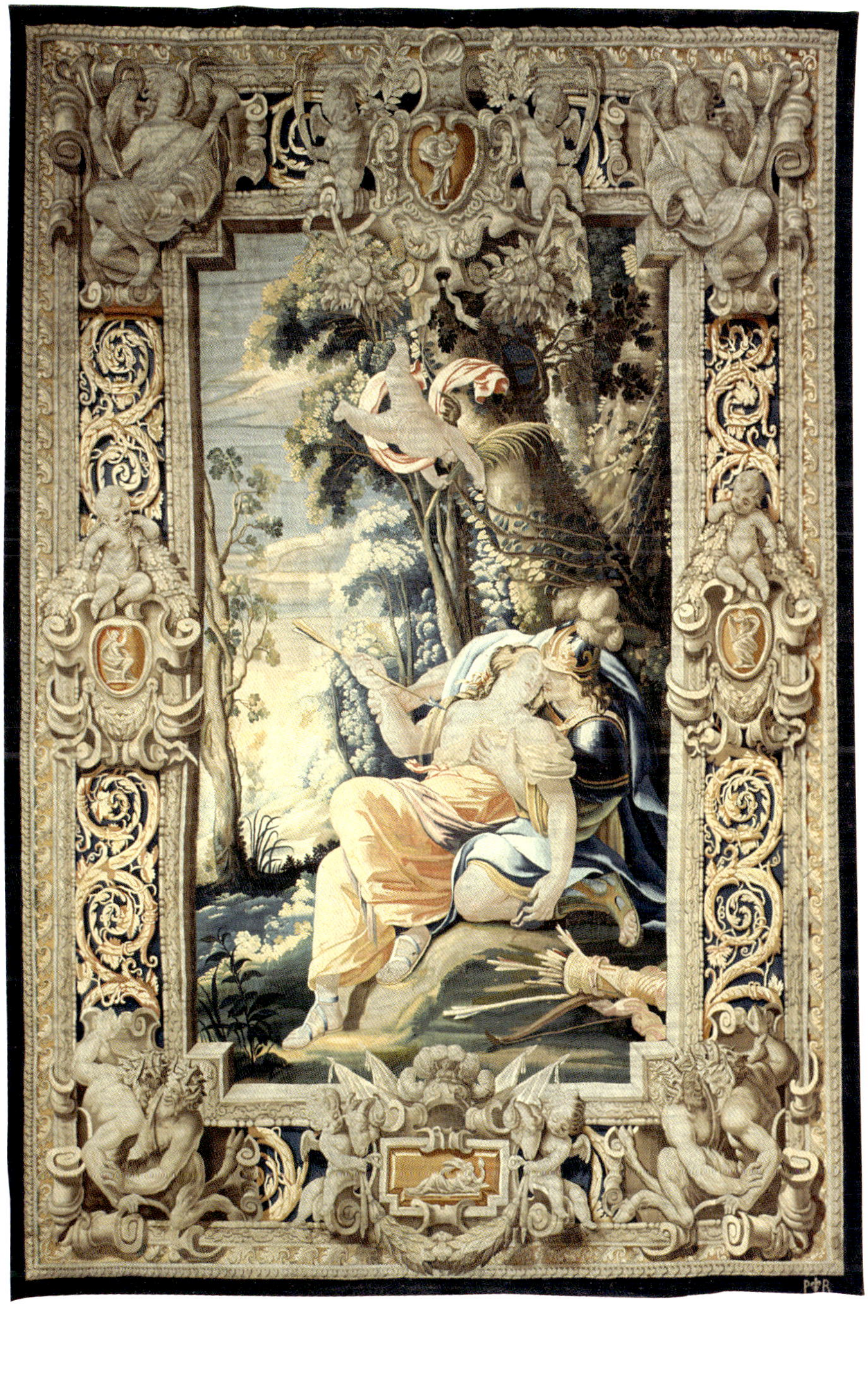

PAUL CADMUS
AMERICAN, 1904-1999

Playground
egg yolk tempera on masonite, 1948
23½ x 17½ inches
Georgia Museum of Art, University of Georgia; university purchase. GMOA 70.2619

Paul Cadmus began painting in the early 1930s. His first paid works were done for the WPA during the Depression. Sometime satirist, sometime moralist, and fervent advocate of the human figure even during the heyday of Abstract Expressionism, he is usually characterized as a 'magic realist.' As he has said, "I want people to know what I am saying. I want clarity, but many times I need mystery, as I don't intend to unravel all the mysteries for everyone."

The time here is 1948, when most of post-war America was flexing its newfound muscle worldwide. But Cadmus' painting is of a different America, the land of the lost, the hopeless, the mocking. This is a playground of anxiety in underclass New York. Only young men move inside the chain-link fence, almost like convicts in a prison's recreation yard. In the background gape a cold, intimidating church and two tenements, one empty and burned, the other with a death's head in the middle window of the fourth floor. Only splotches of sunlight can fight their way down into these canyons to spotlight the central characters.

Homoerotic, the picture shows the bitter loneliness of love rejected or undiscovered. This may well be the immediate aftermath of an attempted encounter, either interrupted by the now taunting group to the right or refused by the dark-haired figure slouching against the fence. The central blond figure, mocked and friendless, stares directly at the viewer, asking for some shred of understanding. Old newspapers, like discarded clothes, lie at his feet. His loneliness is framed by the surrounding images: the gauche teenage couple at the far left, the phallic symbolism of baseball bats, the sad attempt to portray Superman by the boy in the upper right. The directness of the blond boy's gaze breaks out of the painting, looking for love, any love, out of the narrow frame of his circumscribed life.

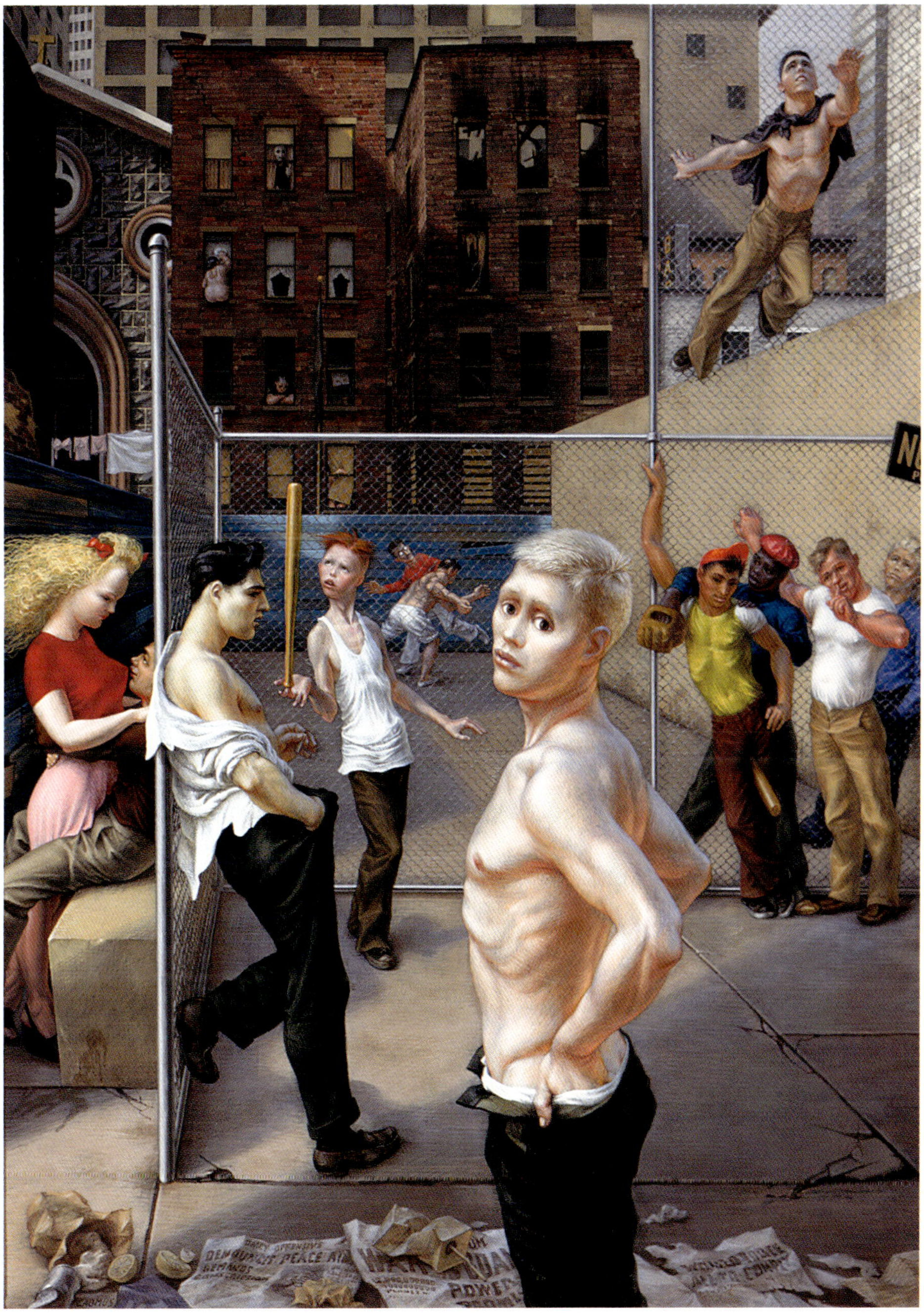

George Bellows
American, 1882-1934

Solitude
lithograph on paper, 1917
17⅛ x 15½ inches
Courtesy of C. & J. Goodfriend Drawings and Prints, New York, NY

17

George Bellows, one of America's great realists, was first known as a member of the 'Ashcan School' for paintings of New York street life. His forceful depiction of boxing, *Stag at Sharky's,* is among the most recognized American images. Later he moved into portraits and landscapes of the Maine coast, all marked by a strong structure and intense colors. Throughout his life, he continued to experiment with new theories of color and composition. At the time of this lithograph, he was nearly finished with a period of dazzling opulence and moving into a war-inspired monochromatic period.

In this work, the solitary single figure, shoved to the far left by the sea of erotic activity in the rest of the lithograph, is faceless, overweight, shabbily dressed. His hands hang down listlessly, while all the other hands are active and groping. Vertical hatchings mark his clothes; dramatic diagonals define the bodies of the others. Many of the couples, lit by unseen streetlights, appear to glow from their own ardent heat — he seems to shiver in the night chill. We can feel the solitary's sorrow. The frozen moment of the image, a game of musical chairs in which everyone else wins, offers no hope but the prospect of further bitterness.

Loneliness, love's failure, haunts everyone. Even those in love are aware of its fragility: a harsh word, a misunderstanding, the sudden blow of fate might plunge the happiest into despair. The clichéd way of presenting it is to show only the lonely. But in this work the exuberant Bellows portrays the world as a nightmare that haunts the unloved individual. The proprieties still observed in public parks in the decade of World War I makes this an unlikely exercise in urban realism, a scene that happens only in the imagination of the solitary sitter. Its very enthusiasm throbs and splashes across the visual space, making the unloved feel ever more marginalized.

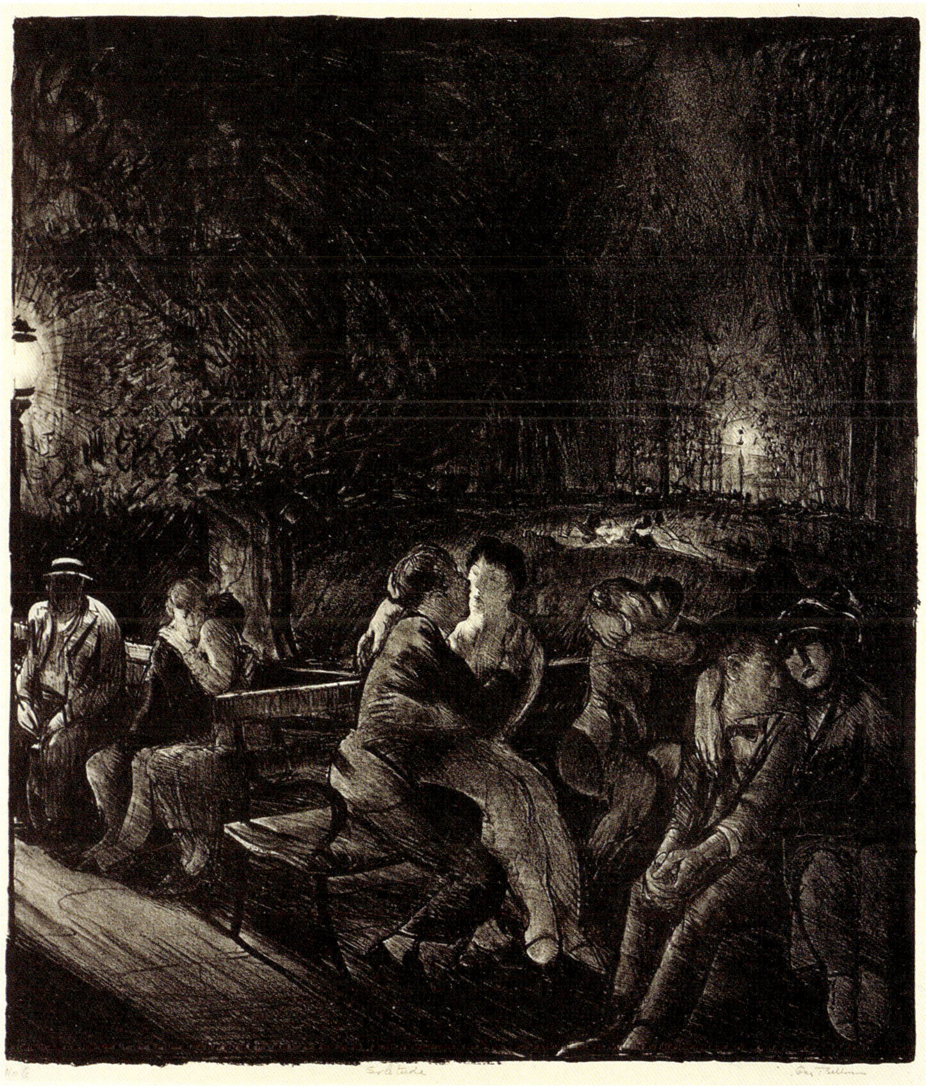
No 6
Solitude
Geo Bellows

PETER J. SIMON
(AFTER JOHN HENRY FUSELI)
ENGLISH, C. 1750-1810

Titania Scratches the Ass' Head of Bottom
stipple engraving on paper, 1785-1790
17⅜ x 23¼ inches
Courtesy of C. & J. Goodfriend Drawings and Prints, New York, NY

Of all romance's aspects, just one lacks time and space: the secret world of dreams and daydreams and imagined play. From such thin vapors of the mind, Shakespeare built *A Midsummer Night's Dream,* a delightful confusion in celebration of marriage. In its magic, a supernatural king seeks to win back his queen while she falls in love with a donkey; a quartet of human lovers split and fall in love with new partners and then split and fall in love again; and the worst amateur actors in Athens turn a tragedy of thwarted love into a slapstick, slapdash farce. This wild confusion of social order takes place under the cover of night, in an enchanted wood populated by Puck and elves and sprites. It is just one night's dream.

This late-eighteenth century stipple engraving is one of the 100 plates of the Shakespeare Gallery, a vast project envisioned by John Boydell who commissioned paintings on the plays from a variety of artists and, for widespread distribution, had them engraved by various engravers including, Peter J. Simon. The original painting by John Henry Fuseli captures a moment of wild irreality in a glorious phantasmagoria suggestive of Bosch and Dürer and Blake. In Act IV, scene 1, Titania, Queen of the Fairies, has been bewitched and falls in love with the city workman, Bottom, to whom the impish Puck has given the head of an ass. She bids her fairy cohort wait upon this lover, and so Peasblossom scratches his ears, Cobweb goes off to hunt a bumblebee as a snack, and Mustardseed ("smallest of all the seeds") stands in Bottom's palm conversing. The text is wonderful theatre, but Fuseli has created more than a dozen other mysterious figures, most sharing their queen's joy. Over all this confusion, Titania with her magic wand, rules, completely enchanted by her long-eared love.

Our imaginings can foster love or destroy it. They can create out of thin air doubts or corrosive envy or even drag love down into the madness of *absurdiste* pornography like de Sade, a nightmare world where no love could exist. But they can also delight. When we 'dream' of future meetings in idyllic times, we can laugh, as Shakespeare makes us do by telling us this dream of love.

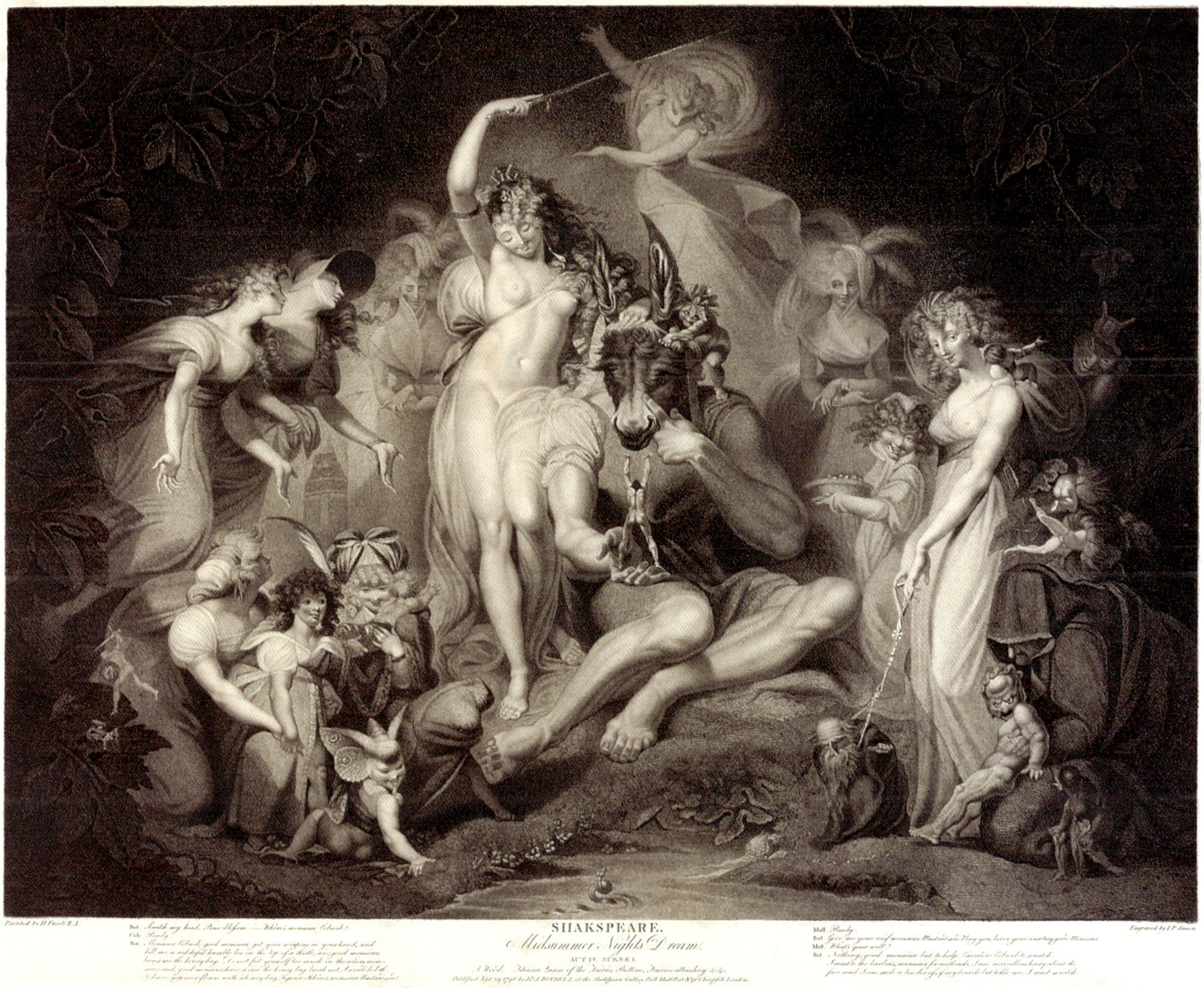
Painted by H Fuseli R.A.
SHAKSPEARE.
Midsummer Nights Dream.
ACT IV. SCENE I.
Engraved by J.P. Simon

MARC CHAGALL
RUSSIAN, 1887-1985

Composition with Bouquet
gouache and pastel on paper, not dated
15½ x 15½ inches
Flint Institute of Arts, Gift of Mr. and Mrs. William L. Richards through the Viola E. Bray Trust, 1962.4

Marc Chagall occupies a unique place in the art of the twentieth century. No one, with the possible exception of Pablo Picasso, has presented his visions in more media: painting, engraving, drawing, stained glass, ceramics, and tapestry. No one's work has so nearly filled the century's years, from first paintings in 1907 Russia to the stained glass of *America Windows* in 1979 Chicago. And no one has brought, to a century drenched in blood and scarred with human pain, such hope and joy.

A tender love is diffused throughout Chagall's work: white brides drift past the Eiffel Tower, fiddlers play from the roofs of Vitebsk, flowers and birds and clowns dance through the air, and again and again, as here, the floating faces of curly-haired Marc and his dark-haired wife, Bella, sail by. *Composition with Bouquet* sounds too formal a title for this dream-like summer's night vision in which the lovers' incorporeal bodies float like angels. A wonderful circular motion lets Bella offer the wreath as an honor and receive it back as praise for her love. White, a glowing bridal white, predominates — a remarkable effect in a painting of night.

Three years after her death in 1944, Chagall spoke of his wife:

> *For years her love influenced my painting.*
> *Yet I felt there was something within her ...*
> *unexpressed; that she had treasures buried*
> *away in her heart. Her lips had the scent of*
> *the first kiss, a kiss like a thirst for justice.*
> *I can see her now a few weeks before her*
> *eternal sleep, fresh and beautiful as always.*
> *I can still see her back and delicate profile.*
> *She does not move. She waits, and thinks,*
> *and perhaps already sees other worlds.*
> *Perhaps, later on, others will come who*
> *can scent the perfume of her flowers*
> *and of her art.*

Has a greater tribute ever been composed to a wife, except perhaps for Chagall's canvases themselves?

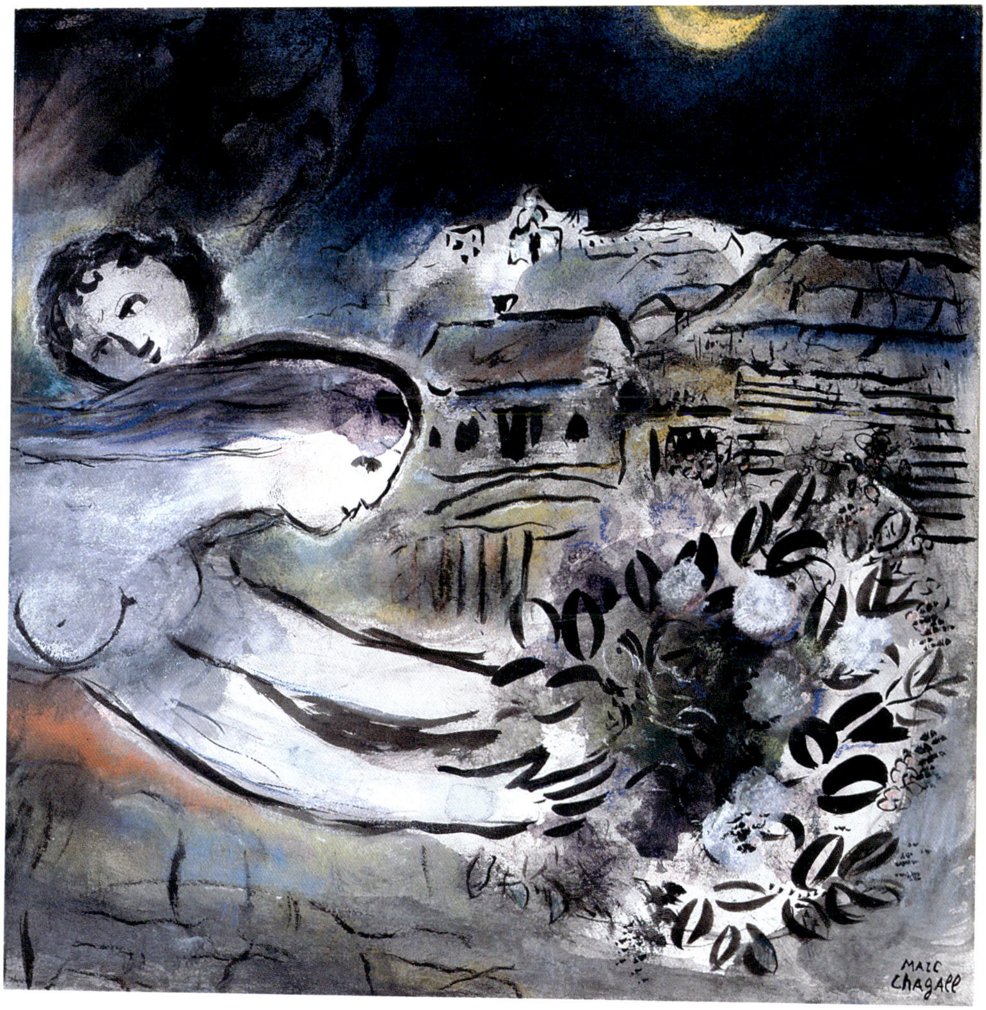
MARC
Chagall

PHILIP EVERGOOD
AMERICAN, 1901-1973

Love on the Beach
oil on canvas, 1937
30¼ x 37½ inches
Hunter Museum of American Art, Chattanooga, Tennessee
Gift of the Benwood Foundation, 1976.3.10

Philip Evergood is best known as a Depression-era social realist, but this picture shows a delight and whimsy not usually associated with the 1930s. In Evergood's bright, sunny day on the beach, all thoughts of job loss, struggle, hard-scrabble existence are cast aside. The ocean is blue as a Crayola, the Atlantic sand as white as a Caribbean resort's.

Gone are the grey, lonely beaches of Winslow Homer — this is Coney Island or Atlantic City on an August day. The lovers may be shop-clerks or factory workers during the week, but now and here they blissfully act out roles as dancers, clowns, children at play. The central woman's face is painted with unruly orange hair and splashes of red on her cheeks and a huge lipsticked mouth — a clown in the center ring. Her blue bathing-suited boyfriend holds her like a ballerina, but whether he intends to launch her in a balletic throw or pull her toward him, we cannot say. Their feet dance away from the mating crabs beneath them, in a social-realist visual pun. The couple reclining on the beach, whose position helps create the central tangle of limbs, may have looked bleakly ordinary on the subway out, but here nothing but pleasure shows on their faces. On the right, two younger girls frolic like putti.

Perspective has vanished in the delightful self-absorption of the figures, the central woman a laughing, cartoon satire on Bottecelli's *Venus*. Evergood has painted her hair the same color, and her girlfriend's long arm is pointing at a seashell. The focus of the picture is its erotic centering, but the context is so full of laughter, there is no place for prurience. The Coke-bottle trash is the blue of the sea. Evergood even surrounds his own name with starfish — the laughter of love in its own world of sunshine.

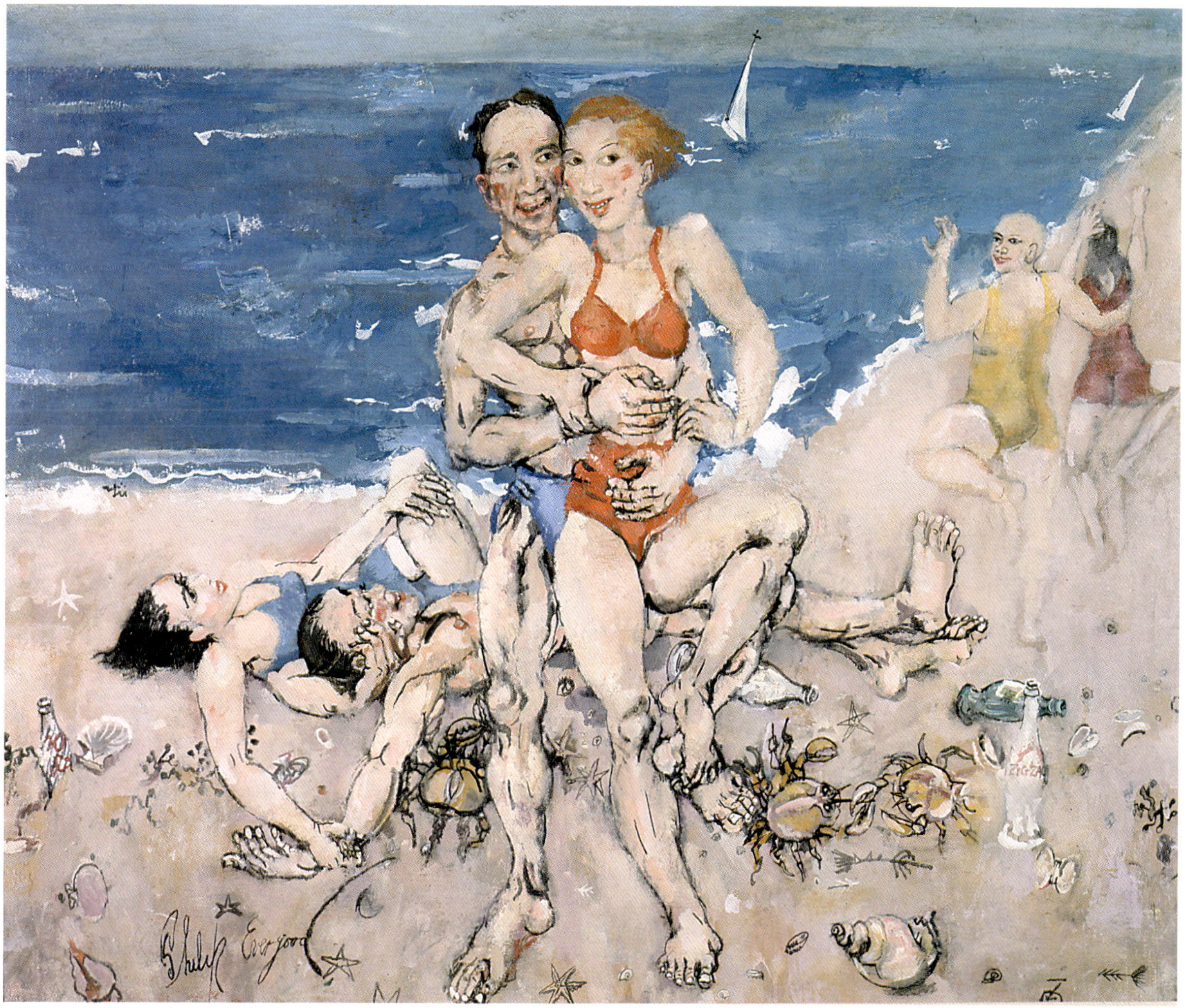

Auguste Rodin

French, 1840-1917

Eternal Springtime
bronze, modeled c. 1881, cast c. 1916-17
23¾ x 21 x 17 inches
Museum of Fine Arts, Boston. Bequest of William A. Coolidge, 1993.50

Almost as well known as Auguste Rodin's *The Thinker* and *The Kiss,* this sculpture was first composed in two versions. In the earlier plaster version, the man is suspended in air, showing himself as the West Wind referred to in an alternate title, *Zephyr and the Earth.* In this bronze, the man becomes more central and attached to outcroppings of rocks. Rodin often gave a series of different titles to his work. Those used for this piece include *Youth, Ideal* and (in interesting correspondence with other works in this exhibit) *Cupid and Psyche.* It grew, moreover, out of work he had done on the figures of Paolo and Francesca for his life-long masterwork, *The Gates of Hell.* The title Rodin finally chose, *Eternal Springtime,* makes the event more universal, less mythological.

For Rodin, form, often of the nude figure, expressed spirit. As the sculptor said, "Ideas and symbols are everywhere; the shape and position of a human being will necessarily reveal the state of his soul." Here, what is expressed is joyful passion, in the vigor and energy of youth. The woman's body is arched outwards, in expectation of experiences to come. He pulls her toward himself for a kiss. They are joined, at a 90° rotation, at the hip. Her horizontal calves, their joined torsos, and his horizontal left arm create a reversed Z, a balanced tension that acts to draw both bodies together. She appears to be awakening from a long sleep. Full of energy, he looks ready to burst into a run. The overall effect is grace, lightness, and a surge of passion that forms a dance of love.

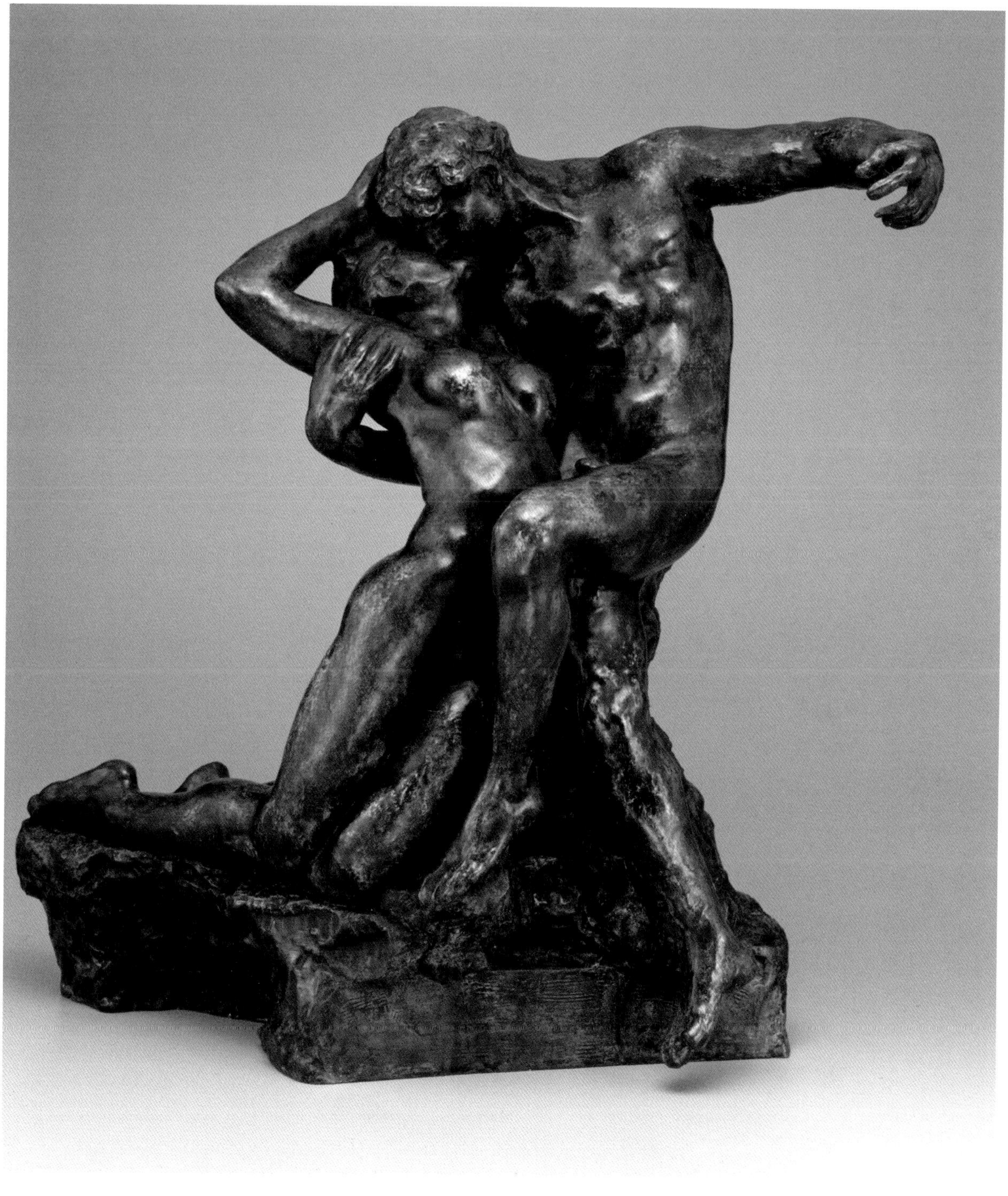

ELIZABETH CATLETT

MEXICAN, b. UNITED STATES, 1915-

The Embrace
black marble, 1990
30½ x 11 x 7 inches
Collection of the Mississippi Museum of Art, Jackson,
Purchase, in memory of Dr. Gerald R. Pascal, 1992.016

Elizabeth Catlett is an African-American sculptor, painter and graphic artist who studied at Howard University and then received the first MFA in sculpture ever given by the University of Iowa. There she studied under the American realist painter Grant Wood. In the early 1940's, she settled with her first husband, the painter Charles White, in Greenwich Village where she met Langston Hughes and Paul Robeson and experienced the legacy of the Harlem Renaissance. In 1946 she settled in Mexico and remarried. Since then, she has melded a realist, non-elitist presentation of Southern blacks with the Mexican tradition of political struggle for the poor. Her work in all media has a strength and immediacy, often with a political focus, but one free of the overtones of propaganda.

The Embrace is not political but immediate. The black marble shows the moment when two become one. The two are almost equal in height and are already joined from shoulder to knee, save for an empty womb-like oval in the center. The faces are featureless. It is, rather, by the differing position of the arms that man and woman are distinguished. The man seems more controlling, the woman more sensitive. The blackness of the material naturally suggests the African-American experience, in which most of Catlett's work is set. Her abstraction of the figure generalizes the forms so they become any woman, any man, together.

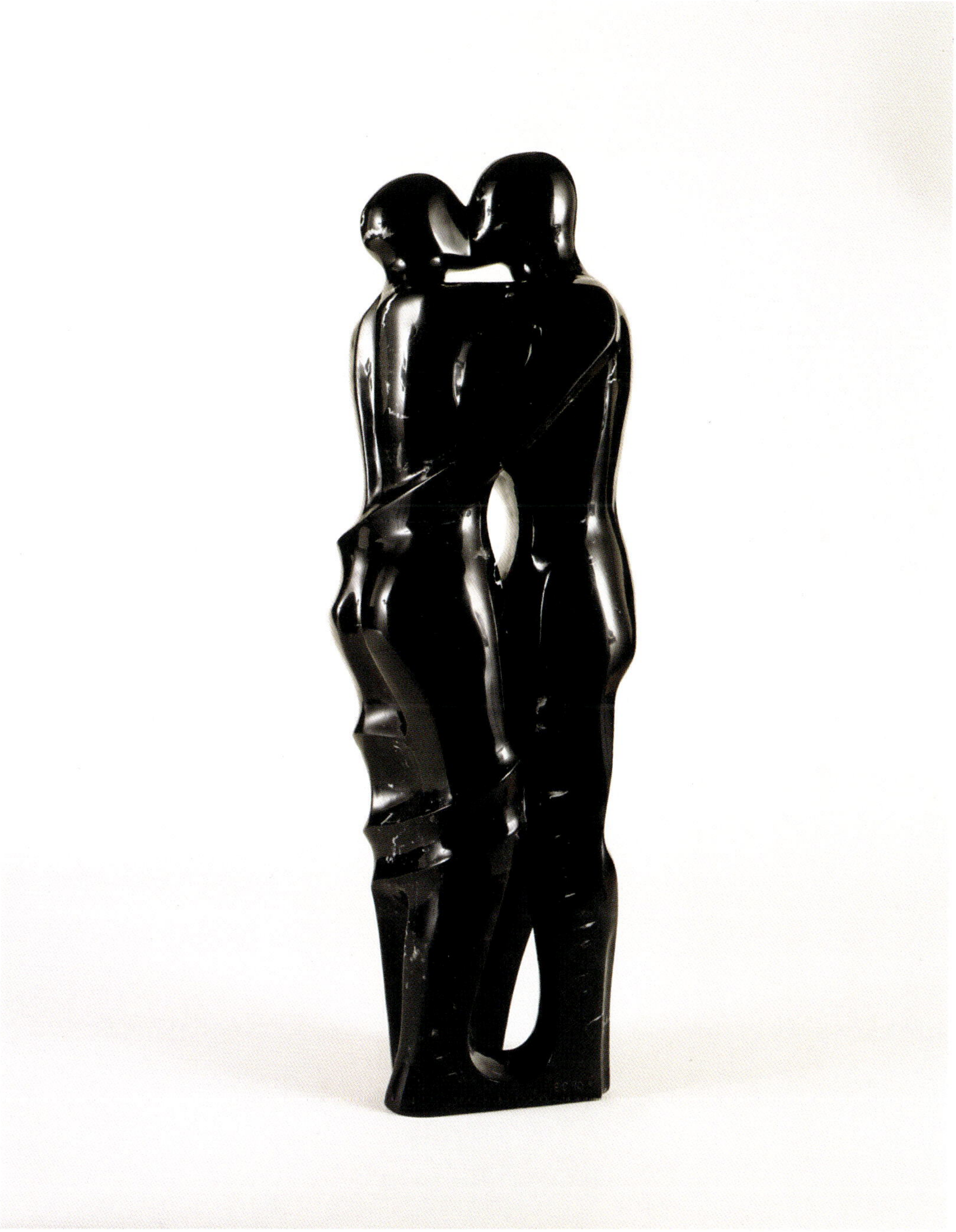

FERNANDO BOTERO
COLOMBIAN, 1932-

Adam and Eve
pencil on paper, 1973
17 x 14 inches
Arkansas Art Center Foundation Purchase, 1982. 82.037

Fernando Botero is Colombia's most famous living artist, a painter whose conviction in the validity of his own more representational work helped him persevere in the New York of the 1960s when Abstract Expressionism was the ruling orthodoxy. He is best known for his bright, often satirical paintings with a flat, fresco-like appearance, but here we have a pencil drawing of the most vexing event in love's history.

As a young art student in Florence in the mid-1950s, Botero met and was strongly influenced by the venerable Bernard Berenson. For Berenson, the great critic of the Italian Renaissance, volume in the figure is important and stands for voluptuousness and sensuality. Botero, who thinks equally in terms of shape and color, learned the lesson well. Adam and Eve, like the figures in all his paintings, are 'generous.' Eve looks like a Mother-Earth-goddess figurine from early Mesopotamia, Adam like a successful, well-fed restaurant owner. Each occupies his or her own space and, although both are holding apples, the snake's prompting has clearly been needed to have her offer it to her husband. Insightfully, the serpent's childlike head slips between the heads of the pair. Unlike Michelangelo's or Dürer's *Adam and Eve,* Botero's are not paragons of physical beauty. However, they do look capable of having the most fun.

The drawing captures an interesting moment in the story of the Fall. They are both meditatively chewing a bite of the forbidden fruit — in fact, Adam's hand has already moved unconsciously to cover his nakedness. This is a different view of the moment than in Milton's *Paradise Lost:* "As with new wine intoxicated both / They swim in mirth." It is as if each is reflecting thoughtfully on the pain and death and loneliness that each will face.

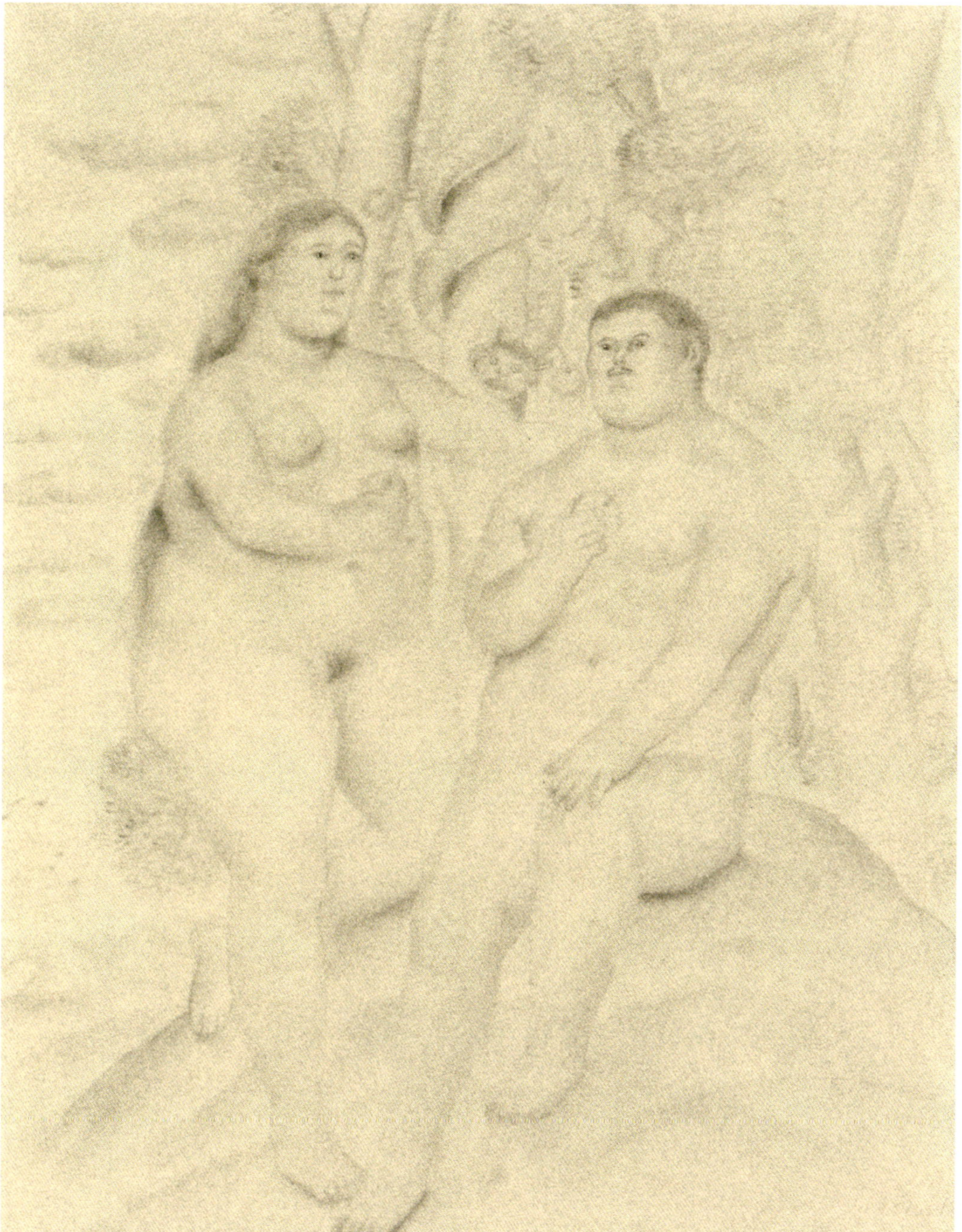

Sheldon Peck
American, 1797-1868

Mrs. Murry
oil on wood panel, c. 1825
27 x 21¾ inches
Flint Institute of Arts, Gift of Edgar William and Bernice Chrysler Garbisch, 1968.25

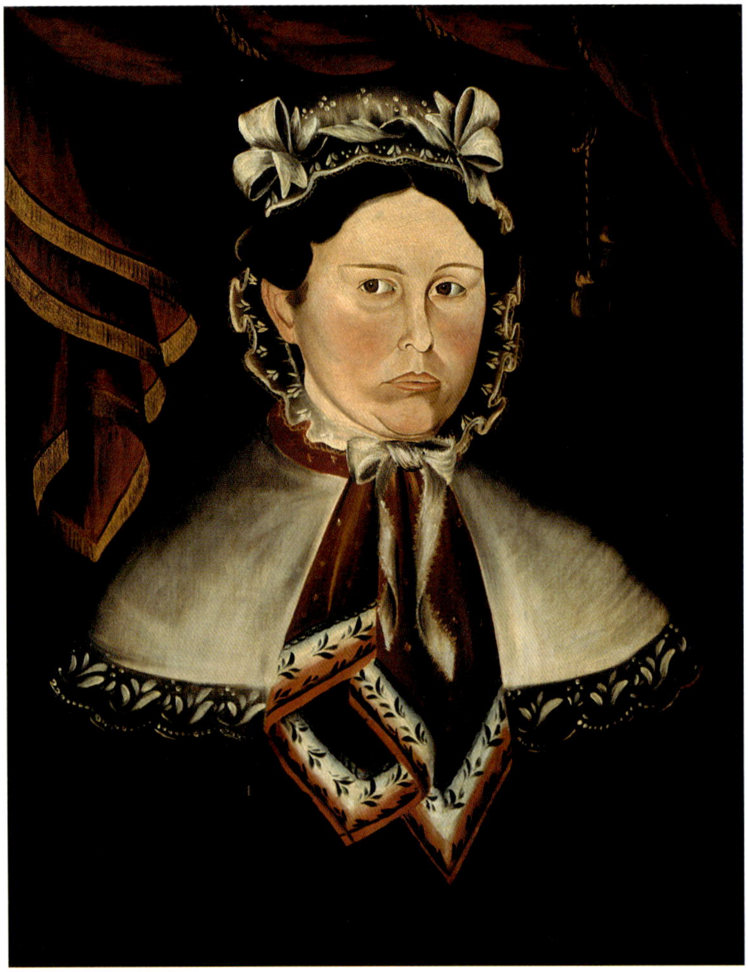

One of the burning cultural topics in nineteenth-century America was the young republic's relation to Europe. Should its art and literature, its self-portrayal to the world, be based on the techniques and subjects of a thousand-year-old civilization or should it aim, as its politics did, at something new, natural and unheralded? The relevance of this question early in the 1800s can be seen instantly by comparing this pair of portraits with Ingres' *Perseus and Andromeda,* catalogue no. 8 painted six years earlier. Sheldon Peck was like many American artists of his time: there is no record of his having ever formally studied painting. This in itself explains the American primitive look of these early works. The stripes on Mr. Murry's waistcoat are painted as if on a flat two-dimensional surface. His right eye is larger than his left. The decorative patterns on Mrs. Murry's dress are an attempt to add visual interest,

Sheldon Peck
American, 1797-1868

Mr. Murry
oil on wood panel, c. 1825
27 x 21¾ inches
Flint Institute of Arts, Gift of Edgar William and Bernice Chrysler Garbisch, 1968.24

24

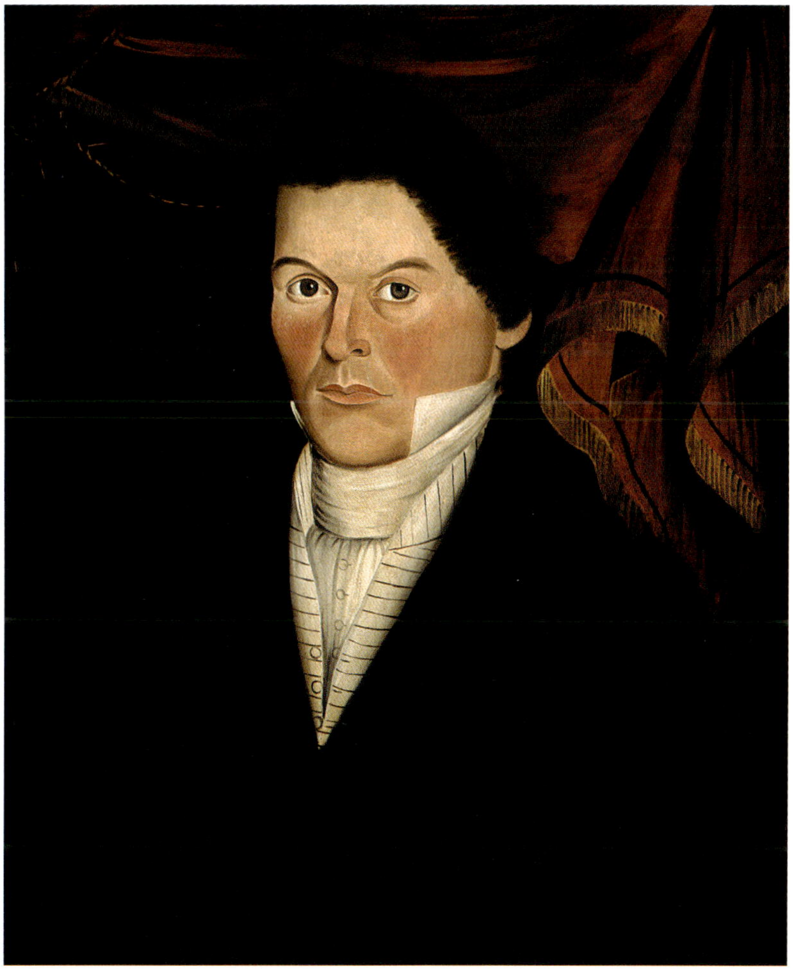

but they are stiff and look as if they were painted on wooden furniture rather than sewn on cloth.

A cliché about marriage claims that over time couples begin to look like each other. Like most such opinions, we tend to notice the few examples and ignore the countless exceptions. Clearly, Sheldon Peck thought this was true of the Murrys. Their heads are the same size, their eyes equally spaced apart. Both look stern and unforgiving in their dark clothes. The notable difference is that Mrs. Murry looks more bitter and disappointed, while her husband's face still retains a trace of youthful idealism.

The mystery is their love. Does it exist? What spark could have flared to attract two people with such flat, stern countenances? The romance, if ever there was any, may be lost in the past or, the unrelated appearance of these wedded portraits simply may be the result of the untrained artist.

Junius Brutus Stearns
American, 1810-1885

The Marriage of Washington
oil on canvas, 1849
40 x 55 inches
Collection of the Butler Institute of American Art, Youngstown, Ohio
Museum Purchase 1966, 966-0-135

When George Washington was still alive the first generation of painters in the new American republic portrayed him towering above his contemporaries, almost like a classical god. His contemporary, the painter Charles Wilson Peale, for example, referred to him as having "the figure of Apollo." Here, two generations after the first president's death, the painting reflects a more human, less monumental Washington. He has the look of a handsome, Romantic hero; curves rather than straight lines define his body. Martha stands next to him, her gaze modestly averted from him — an oddly young, virginal stance for this wealthy, widowed, 27-year-old mother of two children. She is on her husband's left, the customary position then and now. Washington stands a head above the crowd, an historical fact but also an echo from those contemporaries who had painted him from 1775 to 1800. Only God's representative, the Episcopalian minister, is taller; and most of that comes from the platform on which he stands.

The painting captures and celebrates the social aspect of romantic love, the public ceremony in which a bridegroom's man (the nineteenth-century term), a flower-girl, and bridesmaids symbolize the circles of families and friends spreading out from the central wedding pair. The bright whites of the dresses and Washington's shirtfront emphasize this as an event focusing on the couple.

On the date of the wedding, January 6, 1759, the recently resigned commander of the Virginia Regiment was a model of decorum. But the reality of Washington's life was somewhat different. Less than four months before the wedding but after the engagement, Colonel Washington had written a love letter to Sarah Cory Fairfax, the wife of his good friend George Fairfax:

> *I feel the force of (your) amiable beauties …*
> *The World has no business to know*
> *the object of my love, declared in this*
> *manner to you.*

Our first president may have known more romance than hagiographers like Pastor Weems gave him credit for.

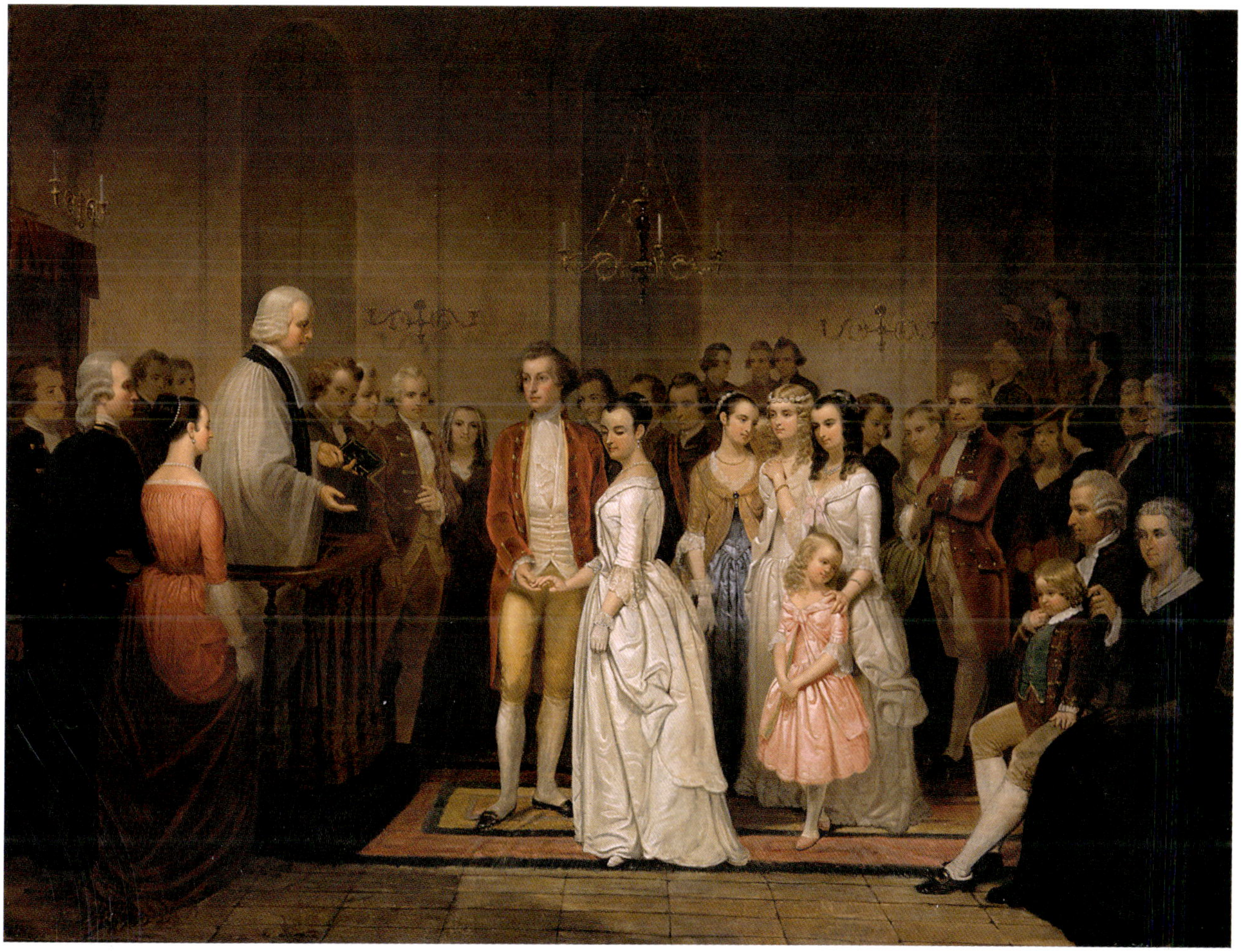

Carroll Cloar
American, 1913 - 1995

Wedding Party
acrylic on masonite, 1971
28 x 40 inches
Memphis Brooks Museum of Art, Memphis, TN; Eugenia Buxton Whitnel Funds, 73.24

Birth and marriage and death are the three crucial events of life, but only in marriage does a person choose. In exercising that choice, every bride, every groom becomes the focus of one day's celebration, and even more, imprints their own life with the dignity of human freedom. In this way, romantic love ennobles the lover.

Wedding Party, like many of Carroll Cloar's works, was based on an old photograph; one of many willed him in 1969 by an elderly photographer friend. There is a solemnity in this painting, despite the informality of its off-center grouping. The members of the wedding party, even though they are standing on the porch of a tenant farmer's shack, carry themselves with the same dignity and individualism as the figures in Stearns' *The Marriage of Washington,* also in the exhibit. "I didn't know them personally," said Cloar about these people. "They transcend their circumstances."

Carroll Cloar was raised in Earle, Arkansas, a farm town thirty miles from Memphis. After training in Memphis, he studied at the Art Students League in New York and later traveled through Europe and Central America. In 1955 he returned to his home and spent nearly forty years painting, in pure, flat color and fine distinct detail the people and places of his upbringing.

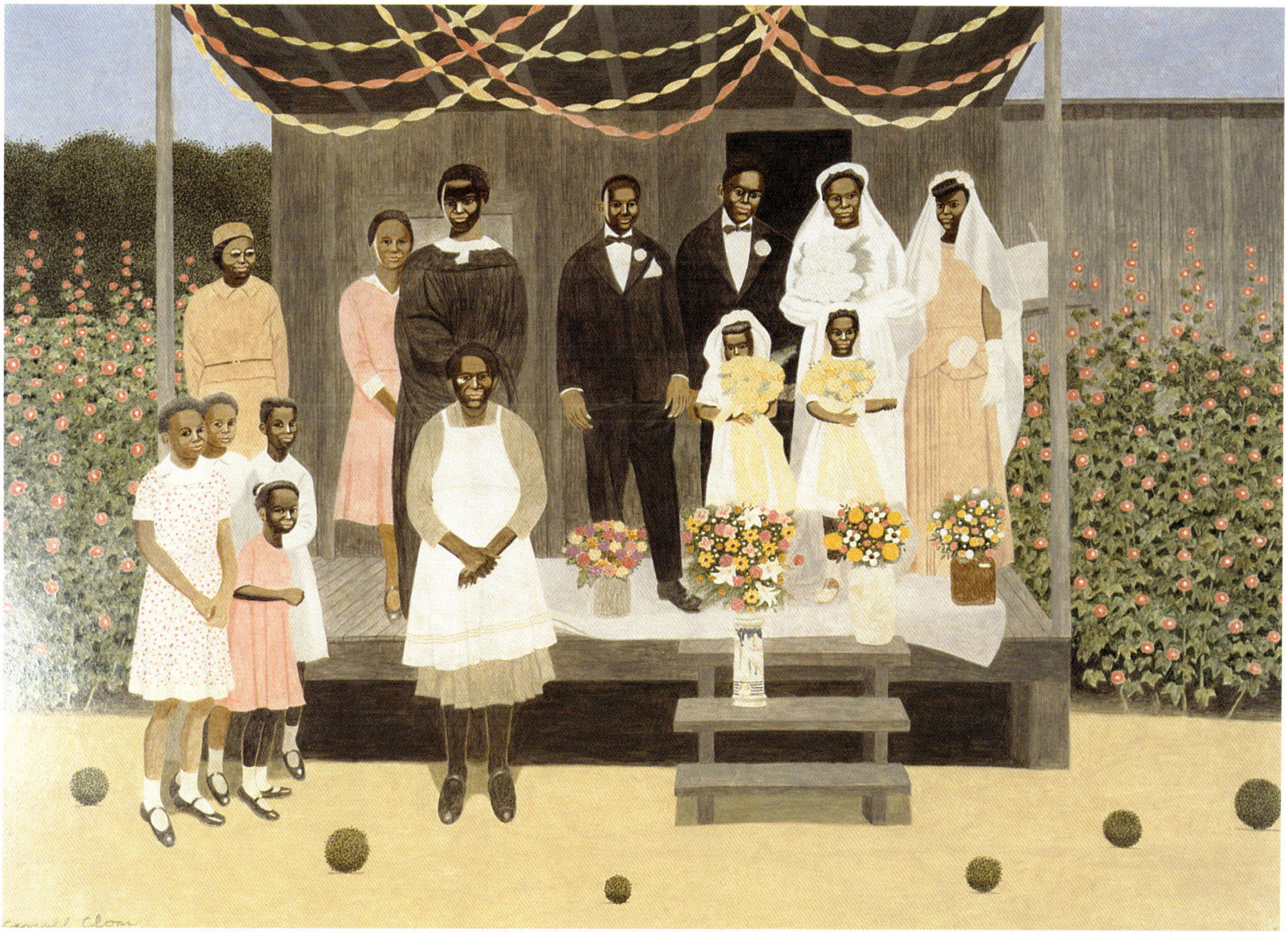

Lily Martin Spencer
American, 1822-1902

Domestic Happiness
oil on canvas, 1849
55½ x 45¼ inches
The Detroit Institute of Arts, Bequest of Dr. and Mrs. James Cleland, Jr., 34.274

This sentimental, prototypically Victorian family portrait might well be titled 'The Birth of the Nuclear Family.' The Romantic movement of the early nineteenth century, with its emphasis on the individual and his freedom and happiness, pulled marriage away from the old notion of it as a social and economic arrangement, which might, but did not have to, produce love. At the same time, childhood began to be sentimentalized as a purer, better time. Wordsworth began this worship of childhood in "Intimations of Immortality."

Heaven lies about us in our infancy!
Shades of the prison-house begin to close
Upon the growing boy.

Later in the century, growing wealth for middle-class urbanized Americans gave birth to the two-generation household and the beginnings of suburbia.

Lily Spencer gives us in this painting the nineteenth-century equivalent of a Kodak moment. The lines are soft and rounded, the colors almost pastel. The babies sleep in the purity of white bed linen. The parents are painted in darker colors; their wrinkled clothes a contrast to the smooth skin of the infants. The mother's arms and hands parallel the sprawl of her sleeping children. Her right hand is raised in a gesture of both blessing and protection. The little ones are a copy of their elders. Note their closeness and the two sets of almost touching heads. Spencer's picture, typical of countless others, praises the comfort and domesticity that was the positive side of Victorian sensibility. There is a completeness of satisfaction here, heedless of an outside world.

Interestingly, this idealization of childhood also reflects back on and seems to validate the love of the parents. The sleeping bodies form the base of a pyramid of strength. The younger child's slightly inclined head is at the same angle as the mother's, the older child's is slightly bowed but looks down and forward as the father's does. The sleeping children appear to be a source of light, radiating back up, especially toward the mother. It is Wordsworth's resolution as well:

Though nothing can bring back the hour
Of splendour in the grass, of glory in the flower;
We will grieve not, rather find
Strength in what remains behind.

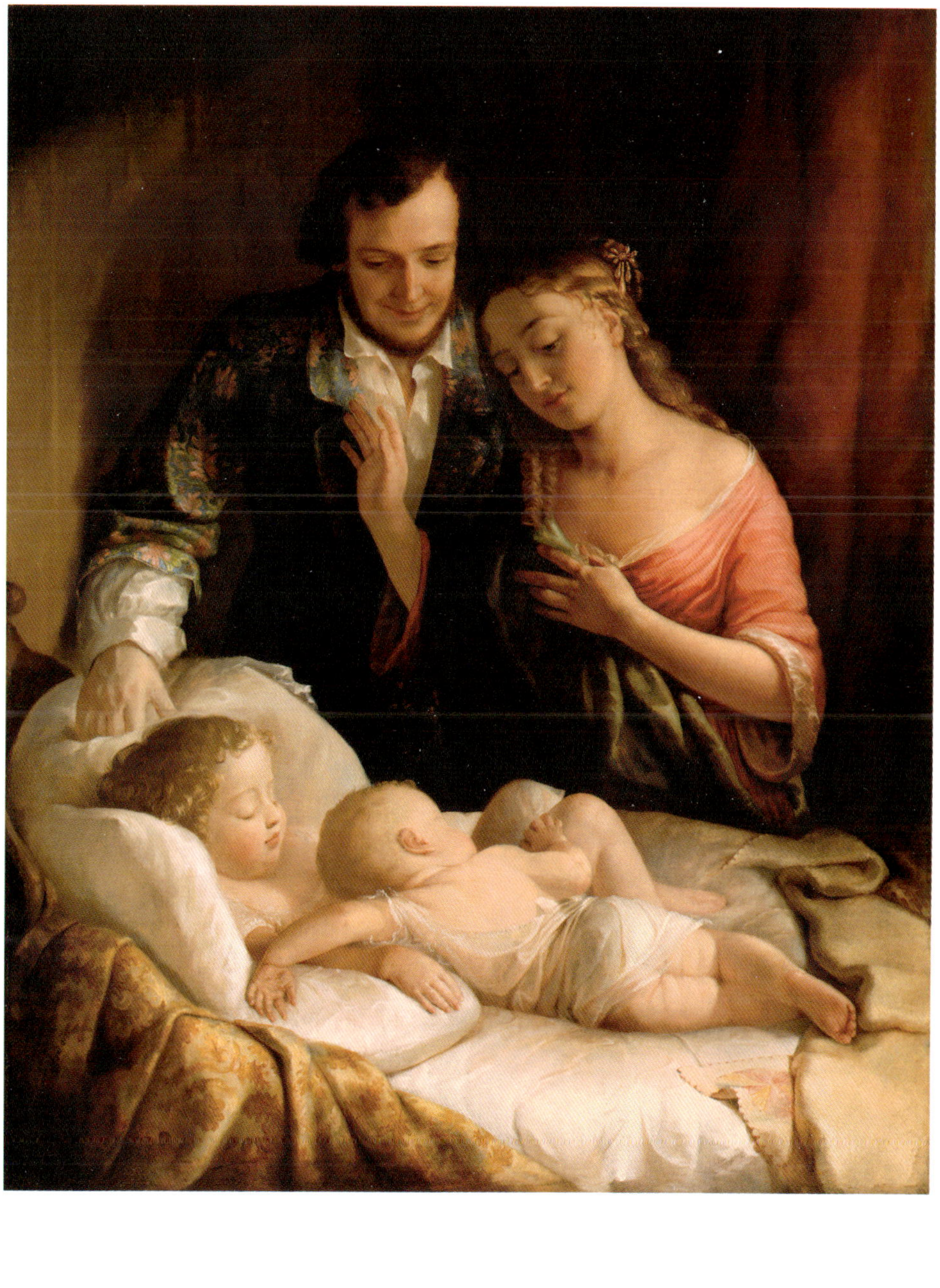

Israhel van Meckenem
German, c. 1445-1503

The Organ Player and His Wife
engraving on paper, c. 1495
6¼ x 4½ inches
Courtesy of C. & J. Goodfriend Drawings and Prints, New York, NY

28

The great social change of the late-twentieth century is not that so many women work — they have always done that — but that so many now work outside the home, with a vast improvement in social interaction and increased opportunities. As late as the turn of the century, for example, nearly 70 percent of French women worked, often side by side with their husbands, with their home as the place of business: farmwives, obviously, but also shop owners, weavers, seamstresses, lacemakers and hundreds of other, often poorly paid occupations. The atelier of the medieval craftsman was the ancestor of these home workshops.

Such is the setting for this wonderful portrayal of married life. Husband and wife share the same plane and look in the general direction of each other. He is playing the organ, perhaps to practice but also to entertain her. She assists his playing by pumping the bellows. Over his shoulder one can see in the next room the still-crumpled marriage bed. A restful satisfaction shows on both faces. Both have the same curved, graceful fingers.

Israhel van Meckenem, a goldsmith by trade, was a prolific engraver; some 550 works are known, often copies of other artists' designs. In this skillful work, which dates from 1495, the year of Dürer's first engravings, there is an attempt at perspective. Sunlight falls through the window behind the woman and helps create a play of shadows. The folds of the garments, though somewhat stiff, show an ambitious effort.

A striking contrast to this setting is the Stone Roberts' *Portrait of a Marriage,* catalogue no. 31, also in this exhibition. There, a couple also works at home but with no co-operation, no sharing of interests or activity. The five hundred years between these two works is a study in the increasing obstacles to marriage in a secularized world.

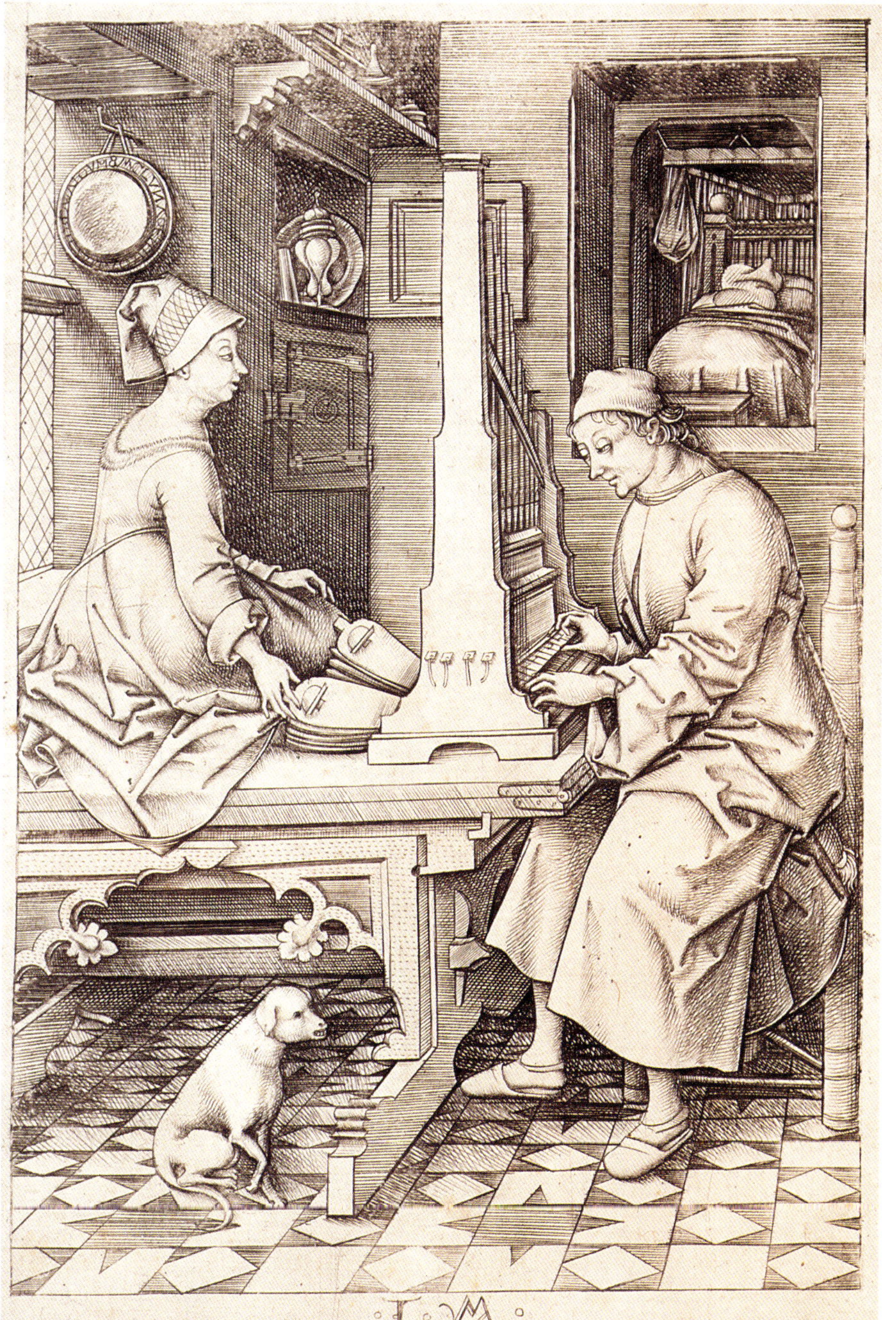

Guy Pène du Bois

American, 1880-1946

Café Madrid, Spain (Portrait of Mr. and Mrs. Chester Dale)
oil on panel, 1926
22 x 19 inches
Museum of Fine Arts, St. Petersburg, FL, Bequest of John Hinkle, 1990.005

Guy Penè du Bois, a student of Robert Henri, became known in the 1920s as the painter of café society. He was known for solid figures with a minimum of detail. *Café Madrid* is the second treatment of his most important patrons, Mr. and Mrs. Chester Dale, founding benefactors of the National Gallery of Art. An earlier work completed in 1924 (the Metropolitan Museum's *Mr. and Mrs. Chester Dale Dining Out*) had shown them in the stylish Brevoort Restaurant; but here, two years later, waiter, dishes, and table details are swept away to concentrate on two conflicting personalities.

The mood of their relationship could be called the blues, both emotionally and from the background in which clumps of dark blue stand for trees and above those a lighter nighttime blue acts as sky. The two figures stand out as blocks of black and white. Her face, in three-quarter profile, is touched with wistful sadness; his, in full profile, shows a strong chin and hawk-like nose, but in a light coloration that makes his heroic countenance flat, narcissistic and artificial. They look away from each other. Her body language goes forward to him: her hands, accentuated by white and black ring and black bracelet, reach out to him but are blocked by the wall of bottles. His gestures are harsh and negative, with one hand jammed into his pocket in an emphatic rejection of communication. Only the two aperitif glasses are on the same plane, and he is not touching his.

The long curve of lights seems to connect the pair; the dots run from his most defiant feature, his chin, away to her bosom, her most receptive and lightest feature — painted in tones of white rather than flesh like the rest of her body. But those lights are in the far distance, mysterious twinklings of streetlights. The Dales are their clothes. Grey highlights on her flesh pick up the softer gray of her dress. The russet of his face is repeated in similar touches on his dinner jacket. They are only their clothes.

One can almost hear a saxophone of loneliness.

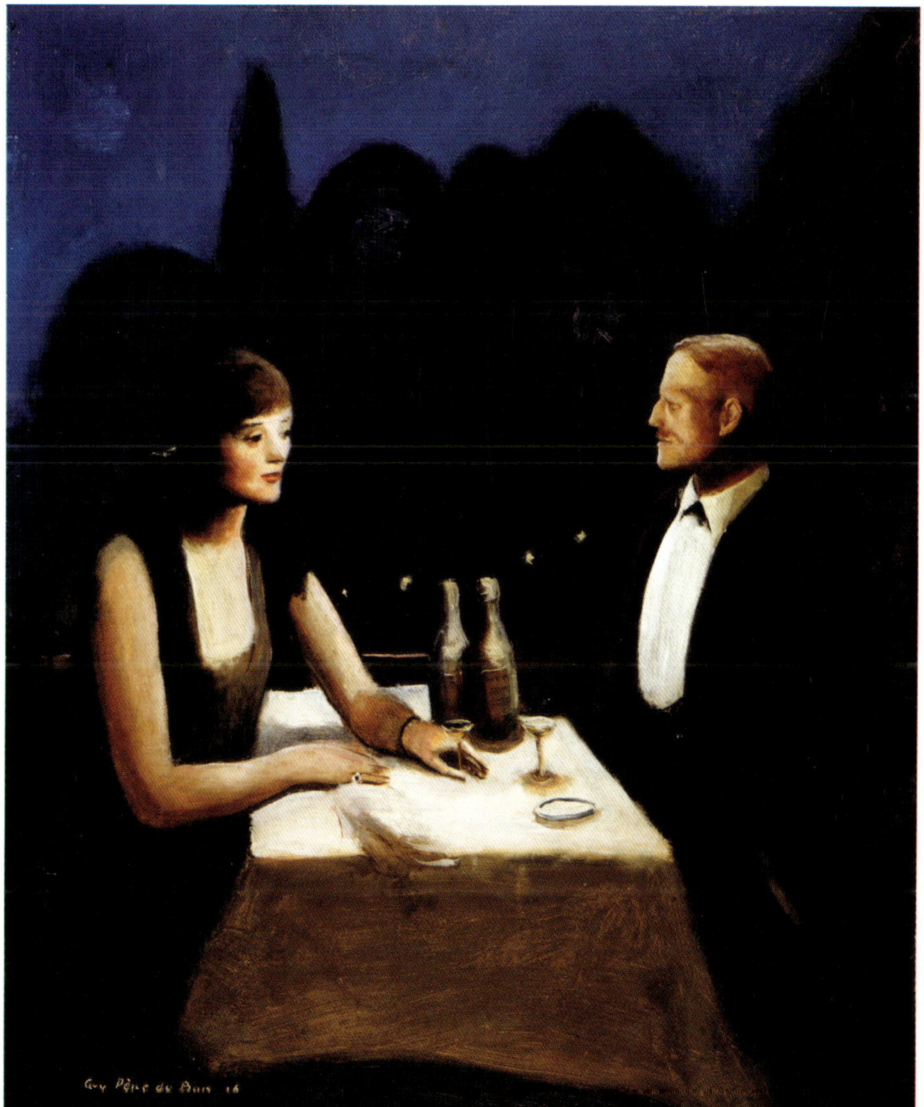

William Hogarth

English, 1697-1764

Marriage à la Mode, plate II
engraving on paper, 1796
18½ x 24 inches
Flint Institute of Arts, Gift of Mr. and Mrs. C.S. Mott, 1964.26

In a series of six engravings, the great English satirist gives us the history of an arranged marriage between a dissolute scion of old aristocracy and the vain daughter of a miserly but wealthy businessman of the City. The husband (Lord Squanderfield, in Hogarth's inspired naming) is irresponsible, corrupt and perverse — a chaser of eighteenth century Lolitas. The wife is a sloppily sensuous, self-indulgent social climber. Here, in their grand Palladian townhouse, the couple faces the morning after.

Light pours into the far room after a night of separation as both have wasted time in each one's empty frivolities. He, still wearing the clothes he stumbled home in, pays no attention to his broken sword (emblem of aristocracy) or the dog (traditional symbol of marital fidelity) pulling from a coat-pocket his mistress' night-cap (a mock chivalric favor). She sprawls in her morning habit amid the remains of the previous night's' card-party but eyes her husband and invitingly extends her right foot forward. She is clearly tired of playing cards: he is just tired.

They sit divided by the hearth, which should symbolize their union. She alone has been served a breakfast tray. They pay no attention to their despairing steward who has come to discuss unpaid bills — this upright, lower middle-class man, with a tract entitled *Regeneration* sticking out of his pocket and with the chandelier above his head as a direct line to God, has probably had a long career of trying to deal with wastrel aristocrats. The rooms show the reason for his accountant's desperation: the mantle is covered with tasteless but expensive knick-knacks, paintings hang everywhere, the carpets and furniture are costly but ill-used, and in the other room, a yawning servant ignores a chair catching fire.

The details of Hogarth's settings add to the delight of looking: they can comment wryly on the scene, delineate the characters, reveal future or hidden meanings, or just burst a bubble of contemporary hypocrisy. Notice, for example, the paintings. Over the mantelpiece is a Cupid playing the bagpipes, his broken bow beside him. In the next room, tall, narrow paintings of Saints Matthew, John and Andrew hang next to a large, horizontal painting so obscene it has a curtain. All one can see of the veiled work is the dainty foot of someone in bed. A line drawn from that foot through the lady's eyes over to her husband shows exactly what her point of interest is. She wants to see herself in that picture.

Ahead for this ill-matched couple (in plates III to VI of the series) lie adultery, the pox, murder and suicide — the moralistic Hogarth's commentary on upper-class excesses. But here, in the more domestic setting of a breakfast scene and still early in this marriage, there is a possibility, if unlikely, for closeness even in this arranged marriage. The more middle-class Lady Squanderfield, daughter of an alderman, still has hope, and may even think that facing the financial woes laid out by the steward might regenerate her husband. But in the end there will be only two self-centered souls — the denial of romantic love.

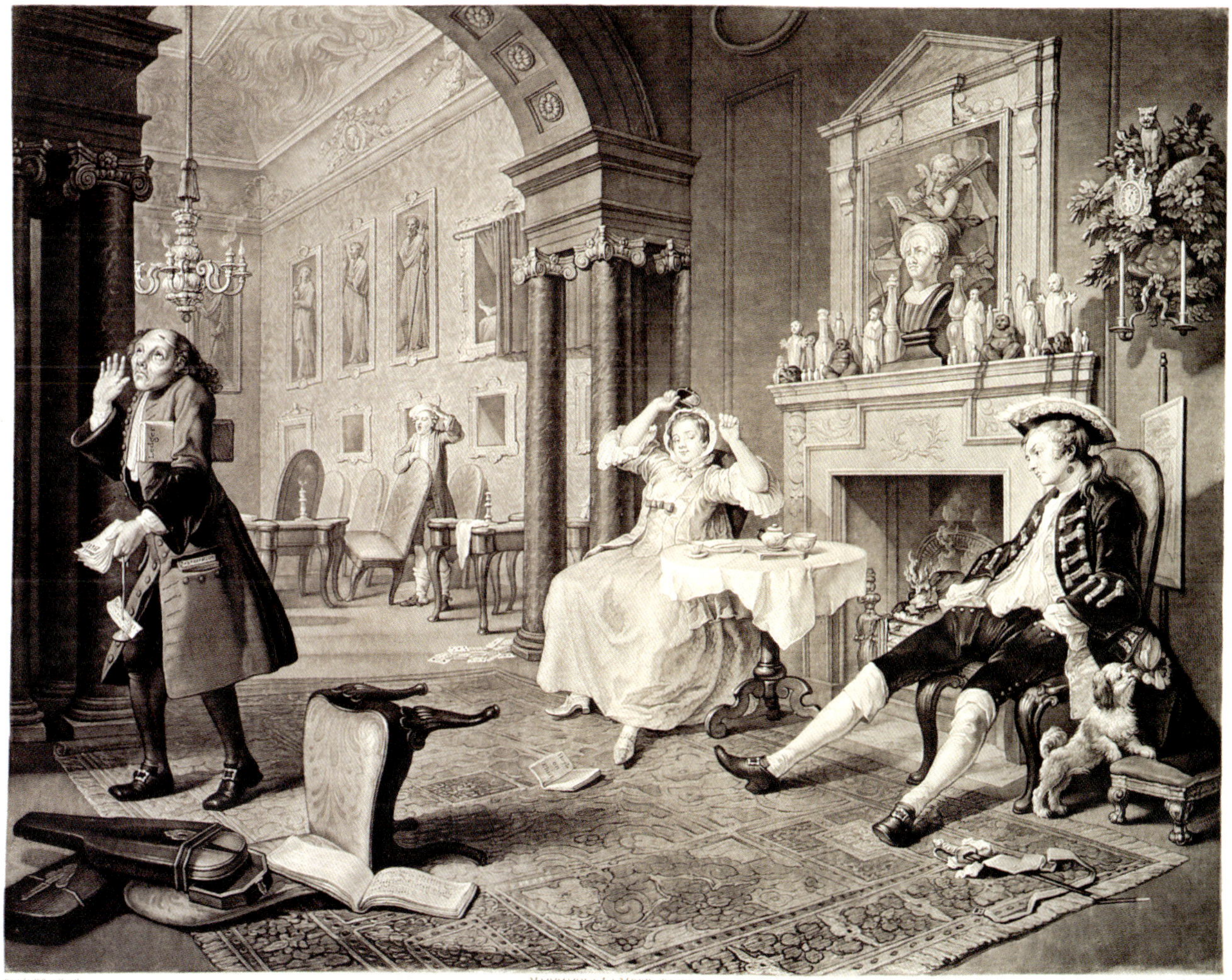

MARRIAGE A LA MODE. *PLATE II.*
Engraved from the Original Picture

Stone Roberts

American, 1951-

Portrait of a Marriage
oil on canvas, 1988
48⅝ x 36 7/16 inches
Flint Institute of Arts purchase, 1995.11

Love does not always endure. Many are the forces that can disturb, degrade, and destroy a once strong love: work's distractions, another's beauty, and self-absorption. Such dangers are clearly portrayed in Stone Robert's strong, bright, vividly contemporary oil. It is a troubled marriage that is portrayed. The husband's body is in a horizontal plane, the wife's in a vertical. He is of the paperless PC world; she exists in a sprawl of folders, address books, and random sheets spilling from the bulging briefcase. Their absorbed glances are aimed in different directions. His blue shirt clashes with her bright red suit, even as, ironically, a blue folder draws her attention and a red scarf supports his computer. Her back is turned to him, but he does not notice.

A contemporary, two-income couple, each focused above all on his or her own work. Her long, striking legs would hint at sexuality if she were not so distracted by some business project. The lines of his torso suggest the posture of a racecar driver, but he is traveling only in cyberspace, handling a keyboard, not a steering wheel. She is at rest, he is moving forward. Their directions are away from each other.

And then there is the cat. In the lower left foreground, a traditional position for the dog of fidelity, prowls a black cat, symbol of laziness, lust and black magic — a disturbing symbol of uncertainty in the couple's spreadsheet world. It occupies almost as much horizontal surface of the painting as the two humans. Its tail's shadow reaches over onto the briefcase, the tail and its shadows suggesting devil's horns encircling her self-absorbed projects.

The painter was a prophet. One year after this painting was completed, the real-life couple who modeled for the artist, filed for divorce.

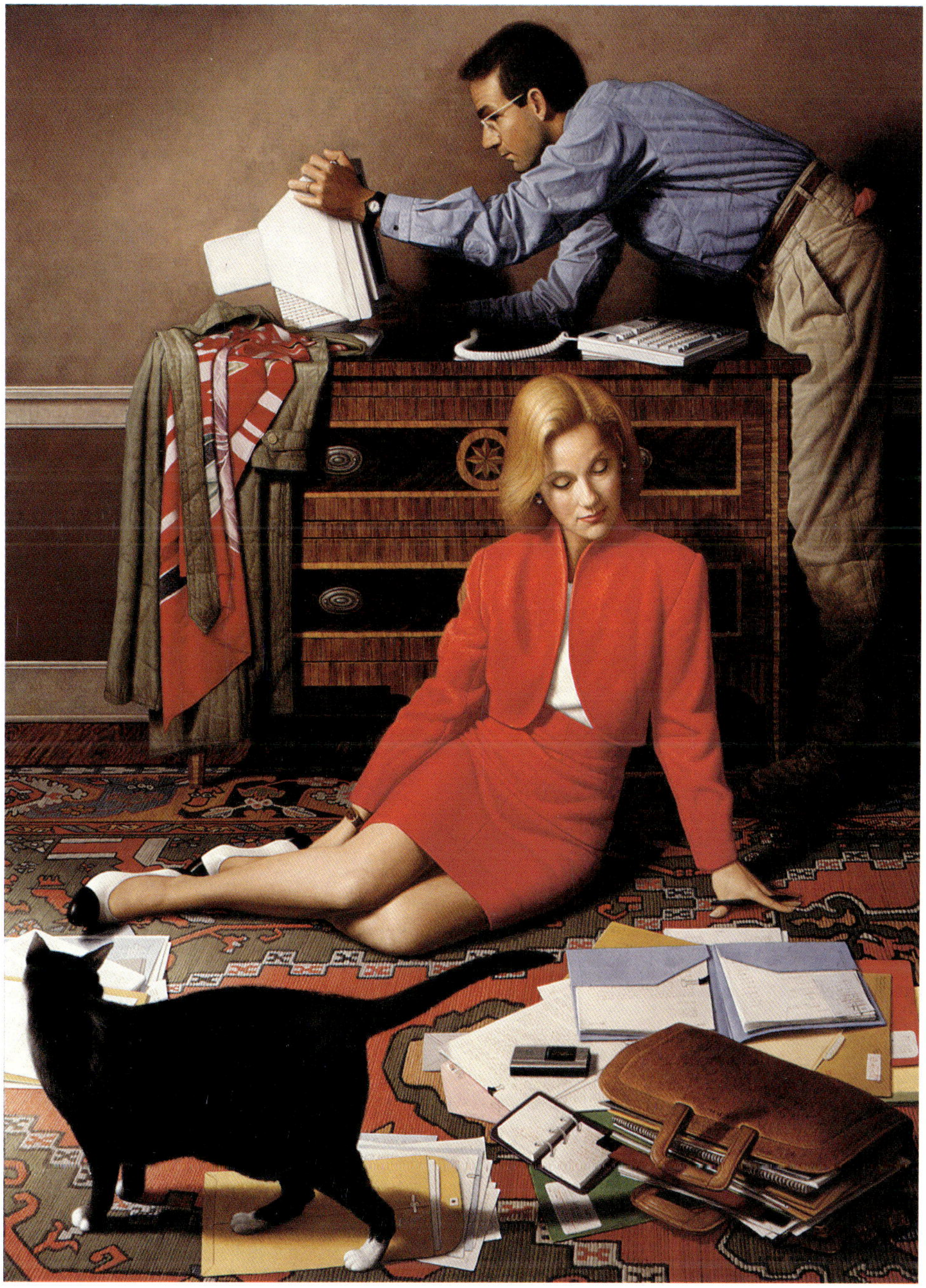

WILLIAM HAMILTON
ENGLISH, 1751-1801

Celadon and Amelia
oil on canvas, 1793
60¾ x 48½ inches
The Detroit Institute of Arts, Founders Society Purchase, 68.159

32

This painting is based on a few lines from "Summer," a section of the English poet James Thomson's *The Seasons* (1725-1730). Thomson's poem does have some fine sections (Wordsworth thought him the best nature poet of the eighteenth century); but "Celadon and Amelia" is not one of them. This pair has no distinguishing characteristics except as the ideal of love:

devoting all
To love, each was to each a dearer self,
Supremely happy in the awakened power
Of giving joy.

They went off on a "tender walk" and were caught in a sudden summer storm, as a result of which,

from his void embrace,
Mysterious Heaven!, That moment to the ground,
A blackened corse, was struck the beauteous maid.

Thomson's lines, though written in the mid-eighteenth century, are clearly proto-Romantic. All the popular elements of the Byronic 'romantic love' — "yearning heroes, pale heroines, exotic scenery, stormy nature, cruel obstacles, and deeply satisfying deaths," to quote Peter Gay — are in this story.

William Hamilton's painting of 1793 picks up on this tone, with its overly dramatic presentation, soft lines and chiaroscuro. Hamilton does do justice to the storm, swirling the foliage with violent lines. But his lovers are theatrical and look like mimes. Celadon's right arm is held rigidly in a gesture from Acting 101, while Amelia's hand drapes around his neck in gentle rigor mortis.

Death in love, death as the end of love, has always been an important element in Western thought: Antony and Cleopatra, Tristan and Isolde, Werther and Lotte. Love, which will never be sullied by the daylit compromises of maturity, appeals to the adolescent in all of us. We know that love will end, if not through rejection then with the separation of death — and still, amazingly, we do enter the dance and move toward each other.

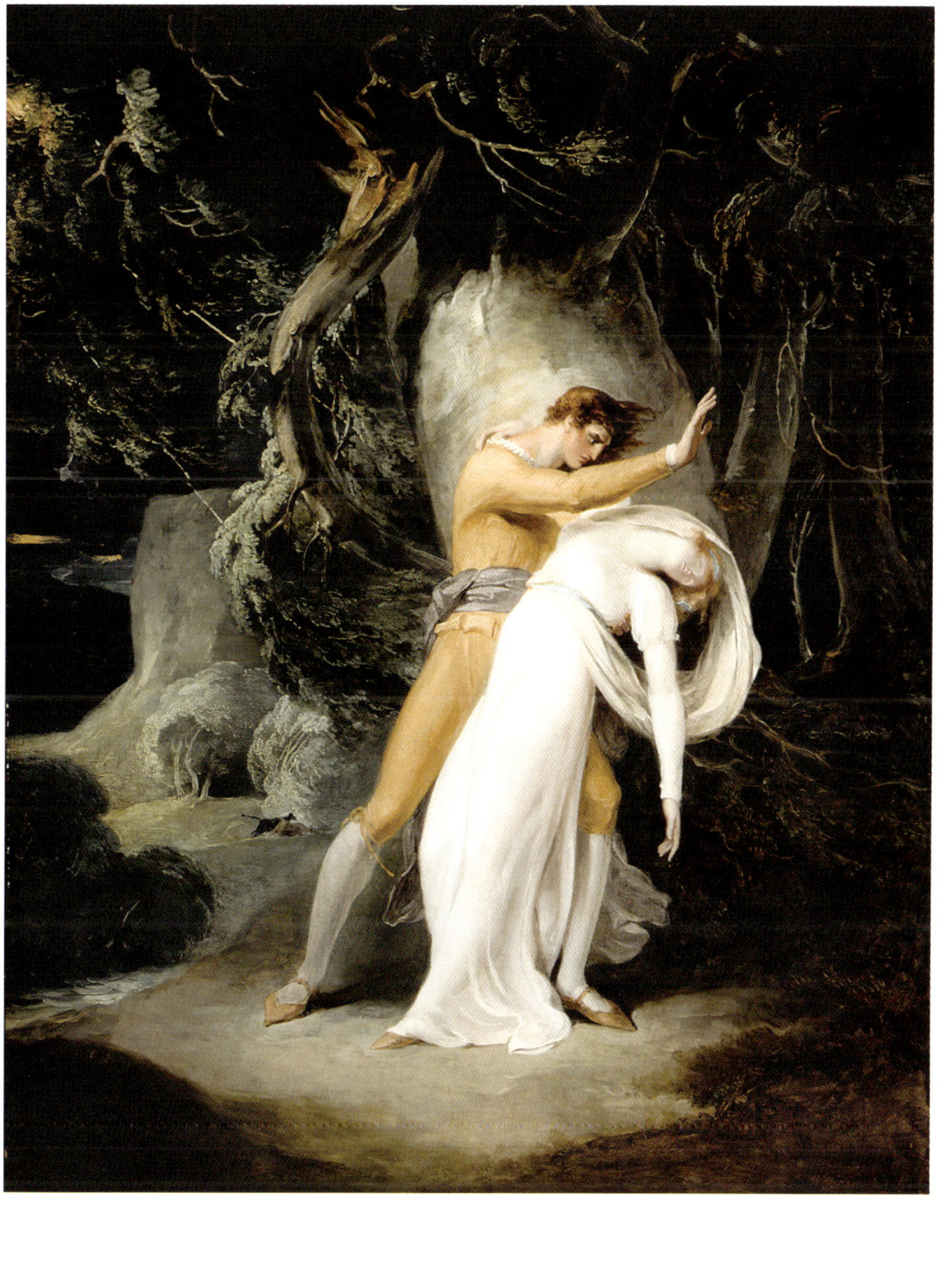

NICHOLAS RIEBEN

SWISS, 1966-

I Love You
Multi-media, 1999
dimensions vary
Collection of the Artist

Nicolas Rieben, trained in Geneva and Paris, "paints" in the new iconography of cyber-culture and video games. His video images are produced by the neurons of the artist's brain acting on the pixels of the screen. As his creation moves and speaks on the screen, the artist has become a late twentieth century Pygmalion, making cold marble move and glow with warmth. We know this is a fiction — the skin looks plastic both in the painterly and chemical sense of the word, the action repeats with the tireless energy of the machine, one push of a delete key could end this image in a nanosecond.

Is this love's future? The unreal world of cyber-pornography and phone-sex — a hatred masquerading as love, with no connection, no touch, and no person to whom we can respond? Such an image could be feared, as the internet's false connection, in a world in which no participant is what he or she seems. Or is this just one more medium for the telling of the ancient story? Since Dante and Petrarch, the loved one has often been more in the mind than in the flesh, more an ideal than a real person. Here Rieben creates, as Ingres and Rodin, Cadmus and Roberts have created before him, an image that speaks to us, as theirs do, and tells us those most desired of words: "I love you." So we end as we began, with words out of thin air, the whisperings of love, words that urge us to move from the ideal to the real, words that offer an end to life's loneliness: "I love you."

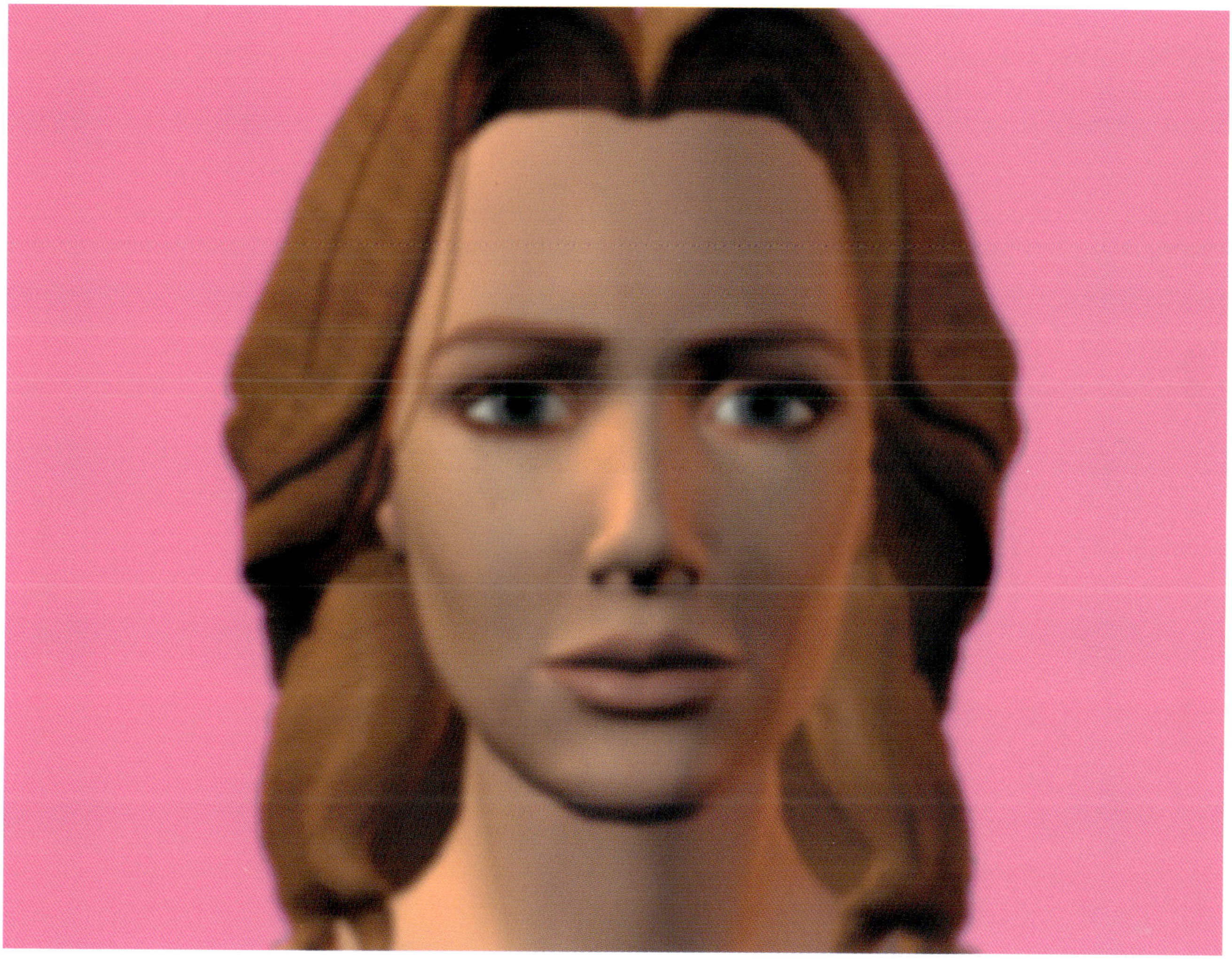

Lenders to the Exhibition

The Arkansas Art Center, Little Rock, AR
The Butler Institute of American Art, Youngstown, OH
Dahesh Museum, New York, NY
Delaware Art Museum, Wilmington, DE
Detroit Institute of Arts, Detroit, MI
Flint Institute of Arts, Flint, MI
Georgia Museum of Art, Athens, GA
C. & J. Goodfriend Drawings and Prints, New York, NY
Hammer Galleries, New York, NY
Hunter Museum of American Art, Chattanooga, TN
The Hyde Collection Art Museum, Glen Falls, NY
Dr. and Mrs. Henry C. Landon, III
The Frances Lehman Loeb Art Center, Poughkeepsie, NY
Memphis Brooks Museum, Memphis, TN
Mississippi Museum of Art, Jackson, MS
Museum of Fine Arts, Boston, MA
Museum of Fine Arts, St. Petersburg, FL
New Orleans Museum of Art, New Orleans, LA
Private Collection
Nicholas Rieben
John and Mable Ringling Museum of Art, Sarasota, FL

THE FLINT INSTITUTE OF ARTS

Photography Credits and Colophon

This book was designed and printed in its entirety by PrintComm Inc., Flint, Michigan. 750 copies were printed on a Man Roland 6-color, 40" press. The cover: 4-color process plus one Pantone color and an aqueous coating on white Springhill 12 pt. CIS Cover. The text pages are 4-color process printed on white 100 lb. Warren Lustro Gloss Text. A blank 29 lb. UV Ultra fly sheet is inserted between the inside front and back covers. All design and color separations were produced using Macintosh computers, a Howtek drum scanner and Scitex Brisk imaging system.

page 27	© Detroit Institute of Arts
page 31	© 1999 Dahesh Museum. All Rights Reserved
page 33	© Detroit Institute of Arts
page 35	© Detroit Institute of Arts
page 39	Photo: Jim Frank
page 41	Photo: R.H. Hensleigh
page 43	Photo: Michael McKelvey
page 45	Photo: R.H. Hensleigh
page 47	Photo: R.H. Hensleigh
page 53	Courtesy, Museum of Fine Arts, Boston. Reproduced with permission. © 1999 Museum of Fine Arts, Boston. All rights reserved.
page 65	© Detroit Institute of Arts
page 67	Photo: R.H. Hensleigh
page 71	Photo: R.H. Hensleigh
page 73	Photo: R.H. Hensleigh
page 75	© Detroit Institute of Arts
Back cover	© Detroit Institute of Arts